Desire Code
Commodore House
51 Conway Road
Colwyn Bay LL29 7AW

www.desirecode.co.uk

desirecode®

A CIP catalogue record for this book is available from the British Library

ISBN 978-1-8384021-0-5

Printed and bound in the UK

Written and designed by Denise Hampson
Twitter @denisehampson

To my grandad, William Berry,
a skilled and experienced
typewriter technician.

I wonder what he'd have made
of all this!

Introduction

Sometimes it's a one-off activity, other times it's a more ongoing process, but most of us are in the business of trying to get other people to do something different. **We are in the business of behaviour change.**

We make hundreds of decisions daily. There're the obvious ones like what to wear, what to eat, whether to send that email and how to structure that report... but there's hundreds more that are so tiny we barely notice we made a decision at all.

With some decisions we need to gather information first, like where to go on holiday, which car to buy and which mobile phone provider to use... and then there's the truly life-changing decisions we make that we absolutely want to get right; such as where to live, which college to apply to, which career to pursue, and whether or not to have children.

All of these require us to look into imaginary futures and compare the implications of our decisions, and, it turns out we're pretty poor at it. Humans are not machines, and we're incapable of predicting and processing all the possible outcomes from every course of action.

The human mind is a bit like a super computer, with two distinct operating systems - two types of thinking. The first type is 'conscious thinking' where we're present, rational and aware of what we're doing. It's slow and deliberate, but takes a lot of cognitive effort. The other type of thinking is 'subconscious thinking', where we experience our world through the lens of social, psychological and emotional factors. It's super-fast, instinctive and effortless, but more prone to predictable biases and errors.

The process of consciously choosing one thing over another uses mental effort. To reduce the load on ourselves and free up cognitive capacity, we rely instead on the remarkable and fast system of subconscious mental shortcuts to steer us through the uncertainty.

Behavioural economics is the study of those hidden forces that influence human behaviour, motivation and decision making. The principles of behavioural economics can be used in the design of services and products to make them more effective and appealing to customers.

Any way of tipping the balance to make services more successful, efficient and a better experience for customers is an advantage worth exploring.

This is the Desire Code.

"If only we could make people value their health more and start being more active, lose weight or quit smoking." "If only we could encourage more people to participate in research trials." "If only we could get people to test their smoke alarms regularly." "If only we could make people call NHS 111 before they go to the Emergency Department at the hospital." "If only we could get more people into our stores, engaging with our brand, engaging with us on social media, buying our products, telling their friends…"

Most public sector organisations have to focus their attention on the things they believe will have the greatest impact for their limited resources. After strategically agreeing a way forward, many organisations create services that are needed, and then watch as they are met with little more than apathy from the people who would have benefitted the most from them.

It happens a lot, and it's a humbling lesson in the difference between need and want. People may need the services provided, but they don't want them, or don't want them enough to overcome the effort of accessing them.

This lesson isn't only for the public sector. Private companies can face significant failure if they don't focus on what customers want as well as what they need. The upside is they can gain huge competitive advantages over their rivals when they do.

Design for what customers want
(as well as what they need)

Applying behavioural economics isn't about absolutes, but there's an advantage when working with human behaviour, rather than against it.

It's like a game of snakes and ladders, with extra ladders

If you want to design excellent, desirable services, start by considering trends that are already here and that will continue to shape services of the future:

What's out...

- ☐ One-size-fits-all, generic and impersonal.

- ☐ Cold and uncaring, passively processing a steady flow of 'users'.

- ☐ Services that meet low expectations, that are just no worse than the competition.

- ☐ Uncoordinated, difficult and disjointed, passing the customer off from one party to another.

- ☐ Limited to the stand-alone transaction at hand.

- ☐ Making the customer do the hard work.

- ☐ Services that provide rational benefits and are price-driven.

What's in...

- ☐ Personalised to meet the unique wants and needs of each customer.

- ☐ Services that are experiences - emotionally engaging, warm and authentic.

- ☐ Designed to delight customers, not just to satisfy them.

- ☐ Joined-up, easy and consistently brilliant at each touchpoint and where the customer doesn't need to understand how it all fits together.

- ☐ Built upon connection and relationships.

- ☐ Designed for humans. Real, brilliantly flawed humans.

- ☐ Engaging and interactive experiences creating strong memories and associations.

The purpose of this book is to challenge you to shape your products and services to be more like this

You can use this book in whichever way suits your own style of learning and engagement. You can follow a linear process, starting here and working your way through each theme, or you can dip in and out at random to any page or section. It's designed to be digestible, even if you only take in a page or two at a time. At the end of each section, there are a set of questions to reflect upon, so you can apply the principles described to your own work.

Behavioural economics and experience design are vast and evolving fields. In a volume like this, it's only possible to scratch the surface. This book aims to give you enough information to create intrigue, curiosity, and a desire to learn and do more. Take any principles and ideas that resonate with you and delve in deeper, find out more, and most of all, experiment. See what happens, adjust your work and observe again. Do it again.

let's call them
customers

There are many different ways organisations can refer to the people they serve.

For most, it's simply the "customer". If you work in tourism and hospitality, you may call them "guests". In the public sector, "service user" is a favourite, though it can feel a bit passive and nods to the large power difference between the service user and the organisation.

In the digital world the "user" is the most commonly used collective name for the people who use the digital tools we make. They interact with apps, browse websites and complete online purchases and processes. The term user, however, makes them seem distant and anonymous and we may need reminding that the people we design digital tools for are human - emotional, socially wired and brilliantly flawed.

This book deliberately uses the word "customer" throughout. This can cause discomfort for some non-profit organisations, which don't feel it fits them. In this book, the choice of the word "customer" is intended to help you feel a dynamic connection to them, and a reminder that even if what we provide is free, the people we serve are actually still our customers.

So, who are they to you? What do you call the people you do your thing for? Are they users, service users, customers, humans, VIPs, guests, listeners, readers, visitors, or something else?

How you refer to them and how you think of them is more important than you may realise.

The activities described in the next couple of pages are designed to help you get a deeper understanding of your products and services from your customers' point of view, so you can approach the topics described in the book with an idea in mind of what you would like to improve.

As the organisation that delivers your service, it's easy to believe you know it inside out and that you know what the customer experience is. This can be a costly mistake. The best way to really understand your customer experience is to actually talk to customers. Ask them. Observe how they interact with your service.

Ask customers if you can have a few minutes of their time to find out about their experience. This doesn't mean casually pointing at a web address on a receipt and asking if they'll pop online and fill out a survey sometime - show you are investing your time too and that you really care about what they might tell you. You could offer them some kind of gift for their time, such as a free session, a discount on their next purchase, or a voucher. Often, just being asked sincerely is enough for customers to be happy to tell you what their experience was like.

When customers talk about their experience, listen out for a couple of things. Ask them what they remember most about their experience. The thing they tell you they remember most will likely coincide with a peak of emotion, either good or bad. It could be a moment of total delight, or a moment of intense frustration or anger. Maybe something unexpected happened. Maybe someone was so kind it made their day. The significance of this particular question is described later in this book (page 148).

Ask customers to talk you through each and every step of their experience, including how they found out about your product or service and how they got started. Make a note of what the customer did at each step and the channel through which they did it.

Encourage them to talk about any hidden steps they took. These are the things they did that you didn't design - the steps in between the interactions. For example, they may have needed to get some information from elsewhere to proceed, apply for something, or buy something new they would need. Maybe they had to get support from a friend or family member. Recording these hidden steps will help you appreciate the true effort and cost to them of being your customer.

Then what happened next?
And then what happened next?

| In person | Phone | Email | Printed info | Letter | Online | SMS Text | Other |

 You will find customer journey tools online at **desirecode.co.uk**, which will help you record and analyse insights from your customers.

Look for additional sources of insights. If you don't deal directly with customers yourself, talk to the people who interact with them the most. Talk to your customer support team and customer complaints department. Find out what people call up about. What questions and concerns do they have? What do they write in about? What do they give compliments about? What do they say about you to others on social media and on review sites, even if it's not comfortable to read?

Often, customers don't really know why they do what they do. They may not know what they want and they probably aren't aware of the forces shaping their choices. As well as having conversations with them, observe them using your products and services if you can. Pay attention to the words they use, their expressions and their emotions. For example, if you sell furniture in a store, watch how people like to examine your products or interact with fabric samples and listen to what they say to each other about it.

This step is about collecting as many insights as possible and it should be an ongoing process. Whether this is all new, or you already do this kind of customer research all the time, caring about the experience of your customers is a great position to take.

And what did you do next...?

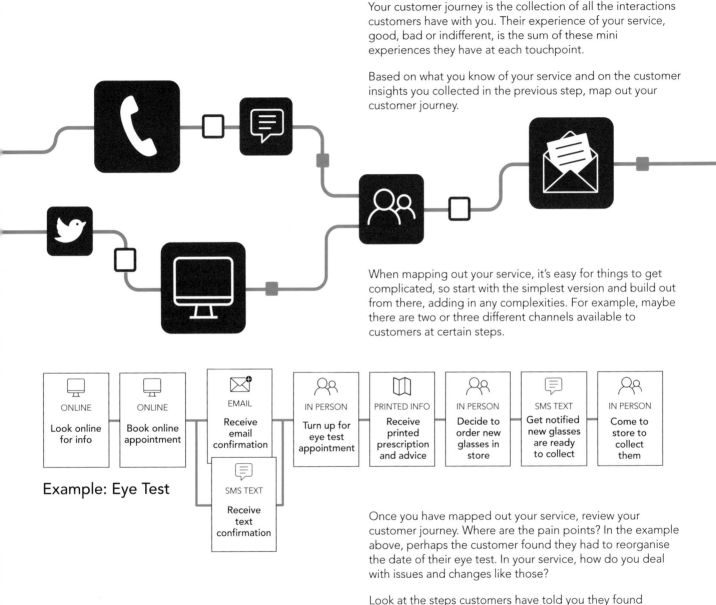

Your customer journey is the collection of all the interactions customers have with you. Their experience of your service, good, bad or indifferent, is the sum of these mini experiences they have at each touchpoint.

Based on what you know of your service and on the customer insights you collected in the previous step, map out your customer journey.

When mapping out your service, it's easy for things to get complicated, so start with the simplest version and build out from there, adding in any complexities. For example, maybe there are two or three different channels available to customers at certain steps.

Example: Eye Test

ONLINE	ONLINE	EMAIL	IN PERSON	PRINTED INFO	IN PERSON	SMS TEXT	IN PERSON
Look online for info	Book online appointment	Receive email confirmation	Turn up for eye test appointment	Receive printed prescription and advice	Decide to order new glasses in store	Get notified new glasses are ready to collect	Come to store to collect them

SMS TEXT
Receive text confirmation

Once you have mapped out your service, review your customer journey. Where are the pain points? In the example above, perhaps the customer found they had to reorganise the date of their eye test. In your service, how do you deal with issues and changes like those?

Look at the steps customers have told you they found frustrating or difficult and make a note of any steps where customers felt high emotion, positive or negative. Are there any moments they feel excited, angry, surprised, delighted, frustrated or fearful?

Not all customers will complete the whole journey through your service. Some will inevitably drop out. For example, if you sell products online, not everyone who comes to your website will look at a product page. Not everyone who looks at a product will put one in their basket. Not everyone with a product in their basket will go to the checkout. Not everyone at the checkout will complete a purchase. With even a small percentage drop out at each stage, the journey through your service will look like a bit like the funnel below.

The aim of your service is to get customers through to the last step. If you are selling products, you want customers to make a purchase. If you work in a public service, like the health service, for example, you will want patients to get through to the end to complete their treatment, to make those lifestyle changes and to achieve those health outcomes.

To plot the shape of the funnel for your service you need to find out approximately how many customers make it through to each step. You may need access to multiple sources of information. Those sources may not seem comparable, but as long as you are consistent with them, you will notice any changes over time.

Your funnel will show you roughly the percentage of customers who drop out at each step. For every few customers you can keep at each stage, the more will make it through to that last step. Even small percentage changes are worthwhile.

Does this information give you any clues to what you might want to focus on to improve?

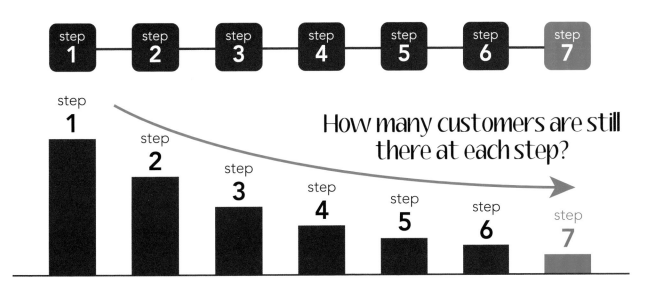

How many customers are still there at each step?

The Experience Cycle describes how we interact with brands and services as a series of experiences. For an example of this in action, think of the process you go through when booking a holiday:

1 Inspire

Before you book a holiday you need to receive some inspiration from somewhere so you can choose where to go. Inspiration for a trip can come from a number of sources. You could see some incredible destination pictures on Instagram, or read the enviable updates a friend posts of their trip on Facebook. Maybe you see your friend in person when they return from their travels and they tell you stories about their favourite moments and trip highlights over a coffee. Perhaps you see a television commercial of an unusual or beautiful destination, scenes from a movie catch your eye, or you watch a travel documentary where a celebrity visits somewhere interesting. Or, you could have great memories of a place you've already been to, somewhere you particularly liked. Any or all of these can spark inspiration, and now that you are thinking about those sandy beaches and hip restaurants, you move onto the next phase...

2 Plan

You plan your trip and do your research. You'll be busy finding out what time of year has the best weather, which airport and airline you can travel with, how much it will cost and what fun things you can do while you are there.

3 Commit

You do the bookings. You commit to your travel plans, pay your deposits, block off your calendar, arrange the dog sitter and start feeling excited.

4 Experience

This is the trip itself and hopefully it's everything you imagined it would be, and more.

5 Share

You become the inspiration for the next person. Your holiday is so good, you can't help but share your favourite photographs on Instagram and Facebook. With your pictures, stories and insider tips to share, you have now become the spark, inspiring someone else to experience a holiday similar to the one you just had.

Experience cycle

Inspire · Plan · Commit · Experience · Share

Now consider the same process for your service

Customers start with a source of inspiration, from someone (or your marketing team) sharing a compelling and emotionally vivid account of what your product or service is like. They do their research and decide that what you offer is exactly what they want and need. They commit, get booked in and get ready.

They experience your service and find it's so amazing they can't wait to come back and do it all over again. In the meantime, they tell their friends and family (and anyone else who will listen) just how incredible it was.

Applying this experience cycle approach to designing services considers all the stages in the whole cycle, from the initial inspiration to the telling of friends afterwards. Your job isn't just to design the experience itself, it's to design the whole process.

The experience has to be brilliant, so that people will want to repeat it over and over again. It can't be ordinary. Brilliant only.

It has to be memorable and include key moments people can easily share with others.

Persuading other people to experience something we enjoyed gives us social currency - it makes us feel that what we do is desirable in the eyes of others. It makes us look good and makes us more likely to want to return and do it all over again.

The key to the cycle is memory. You are helping your customers create great memories they will want to treasure, repeat and share.

This isn't experience design. It's memory design.

Desire Code takes behavioural economics principles and distils them into five themes. The first four are concerned with making your service more desirable, more wantable - to raise demand and keep customer motivation high. The fifth is concerned with making it easier for customers. It works alongside the other four, and is essential for creating enduring customer engagement.

In this book, each theme is introduced in turn, along with examples and a checklist to help you quickly generate a long list of possible ideas to improve your products and services for your customers.

Emotional

People are more persuaded by an emotional message than a rational one.

PAGES 15-50

Short term

People prefer things they can have now over things they can have in the future.

PAGES 51-88

Certain

People prefer things they can definitely have over things they may or may not get.

PAGES 89-124

Positive

People prefer to work towards the things they want than away from the things they don't want.

PAGES 125-164

Simplified

To really engage with customers, services need to be desirable... and easy to access.

PAGES 165-202

Emotional

People are more persuaded
by an emotional message
than a rational one

The Ballroom Experience

How big is the dance floor in the Blackpool Tower ballroom?

According to its official programme, the dance floor of the famous ballroom at Blackpool Tower has over 30,000 floor tiles. As impressive as this sounds, if we were to try to use that information to figure out how big the dance floor is, we'd find there's a detail missing – the size of the floor tiles.

They vary in size but most are rectangular and approximately 30cm x 10cm.

So that's 30,000 x 30cm x 10cm.

Got it?

Even armed with the above fact, it's likely that you would still struggle to visualise the space.

Apparently, over 500 people can dance on it at once – but it doesn't say the kind of dance they could do all together or how much space they would use.

It's 100ft x 120ft in size, which is big. It's the biggest ballroom in Britain!

The facts above are interesting but they can't begin to communicate the sheer scale, beauty and grandeur of the Victorian "Paris-opera-house -inspired" ballroom or what it might feel like to be there. Facts alone don't adequately describe the experience.

How big is a five-billion calorie pile of sugar?

The UK Department of Health published a strategic report in 2011 on combating England's obesity problem[1]. According to the people with calculators and spreadsheets, the people of England were collectively eating a whopping five billion calories a day too many. This number reverberated around the newsrooms and in print. "Five Billion Calories" was the bold headline on the front pages of several of the UK's national papers, but as impressive as it sounds it's just a very big number that none of us can really get our heads around.

So how much is five billion calories? What does it actually look like?

To put this number into context - it's about 1,290,000 x 1kg bags of granulated white sugar. Now let's visualise it so you can appreciate better how much sugar that actually is. We all know what the Empire State Building in New York City looks like. Even if you've not been there personally, you've surely seen it on the TV, in movies and magazines. It's 86 floors high, widest at the bottom and narrows in stages going up. If we filled it up with 1,290,000 bags of sugar, how high up the 86 floors do you think five billion calories worth of sugar would go? For fun, the answer is overleaf.

Knowing what it would look like as a big pile of sugar still doesn't bring the message home because the number is impersonal. How much are each of us individually expected to contribute to fixing the five billion calorie problem? What does it mean on a personal level? Telling us we collectively eat five billion calories a day too many hasn't made (and won't make) one bit of difference to us because it doesn't make us feel anything.

Five billion calories a day is about one chocolate digestive biscuit per day per person in England. You may not change your eating habits but at least you'll understand better what the number means at an individual level. And maybe, maybe, if you have found you have a habit of eating a chocolate digestive with your afternoon cuppa each day, you might pause for a micro-second before you eat your next one.

If you want to persuade people to change behaviour, any information you give has to be as personalised, individual and easy to conceptualise as possible. Build a story around it too if you can. Staggeringly big-sounding data may look great in print and on powerpoint slides, but it won't make a difference to what we do.

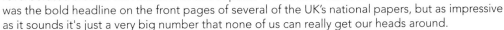

BREAKING NEWS

LIVE NEWS

5 BILLION CALORIES
We're eating five billion calories a day too many

BRK **TODAY** Now you know that, you do something about it, yeah?

Did you know...?

A leaflet in a GP practice reads *"Did you know that 10,000 people in Wales die every year from Coronary Heart Disease?"*

The first impression is that this is probably not quite true, because 10,000 is a round number, but it also requires some interpretation. Is it a lot or not? You would assume it is, or someone wouldn't have gone to the trouble of producing the leaflet.

The headline statement is designed to make us think, "wow, that's a lot!" but that's more about the way it is phrased, rather than the actual number. We would probably feel the same if it was 20,000 or 50,000, or indeed if it was 2,000.

The message in the leaflet is compounded by further numerical information… only 53% of the population in Wales do the government-recommended level of physical activity[2] (150 minutes per week at a moderate intensity), which would significantly reduce the risk of developing coronary heart disease, cancer, strokes, diabetes and other long-term conditions by their relative percentages… more numbers.

Answering the second question...

"Do 150 minutes of moderate intensity physical activity each week…" is an example of a message that answers the second question. Nobody ever asks "how much should I do?" and "how hard should I workout?" without first asking "why should I even bother?"

The first question is one of these...

- "Why should I want to do it?"

- "What difference will it make to my world?"

First question: **Why?**

Second question: **How?**

Behaviour change can be hard and requires persistence, so people need to really want to succeed. Therefore, they need a seriously good reason to try.

The answer to the first question of why people really want to make a change is almost always an emotional one. We are inspired to change our behaviour for reasons that aren't usually based on facts and logic, but which are about how we feel, how we imagine it would feel to succeed, how we hope it will improve our lives, boost our self-esteem and resolve our frustrations and discontentment.

Once customers have decided they want it enough, then you can tell them how often and how hard!

From the previous page...

How high up the Empire State Building?

The answer is 0 floors. The sugar pile would only be 3m high.

Yep, it's a rubbish visual, and will win you no new admirers if you share it as a fact at your next party.

But you were still curious, weren't you?

This high ➔

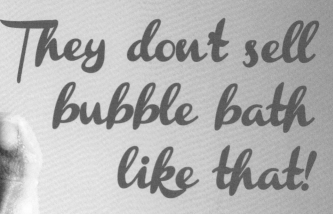

They don't sell bubble bath like that!

Lifestyle brands don't sell their products using a bullet list of *'benefits'*...

Bubble bath:

☐ It smells of flowers.

☐ It will get you clean.

☐ In every 500ml bottle there are about 13 bath fulls.

No, they talk about the indulgent experience of letting all your worries float away...

TASK: watch a commercial TV station for an evening and note how many commercials use emotional messages and stories to sell their products and services.

On the previous page, we considered a reference to 10,000 people in a fact about coronary heart disease.

How would you help someone to understand what 10,000 people really feels like, so that the number has more emotional impact and therefore creates an emotional rather than rational response?

You could compare 10,000 people to the capacity of somewhere you know, so you can visualise all the people at once. What is the size of your local football stadium, indoor arena or the population of a small town nearby?

10,000 people is what you'd roughly expect to find at a concert in the SECC Glasgow, Wembley Arena, Newcastle Metro and the Liverpool Echo Arena. That suddenly feels like a lot more people. The mental image of a 10,000 capacity crowd on their feet at a rock concert has more impact than the number on its own.

What does 10,000 people feel like?

We think in pictures

How do you feel when you hear about...?

- An ambulance trust achieving its Category A response targets.

- The average SAT score of seven-year-old pupils in a primary school.

- A 6% rise in hospital bed demand.

- The tonnes of CO2 emissions from a city at night, or a four-hour flight.

- A 12% reduction in the amount of waste going to landfill.

- A 3% efficiency savings requirement.

It's hard to visualise.

Instead, people think in images. "Imagine if...", "picture this...", "remember when..." Using images alongside information helps people to connect to the message and creates greater emotional impact.

Our dual-system minds

As described in Daniel Kahneman's ground-breaking book, "Thinking Fast and Slow"[3], we have two operating systems in our minds: the conscious (rational) and the subconscious (emotional).

The conscious mind is intelligent and careful. It's a logical processor that works with rational arguments, understands numbers and interprets words. It calculates, compares and plans, and it's the "head" in the "head vs heart" we often refer to. Of the two sides of the mind, it's relatively slow and clunky, and requires mental effort.

The subconscious, in comparison, is a supercomputer, and it processes the simultaneous stream of information from our senses, is responsible for unconsciously maintaining our body systems, and controls our emotions and instincts. It's super-fast and delivers snap intuitive judgements. By its definition, we don't have direct access to the subconscious - but we definitely feel its effects.

Emotional

Excited   Anxious   Hungry   Thirsty
In Pain   Drunk   Depressed   Angry
Upset   Disatisfied   Frustrated
Inspired   Scared
Too hot or cold

Rational

Pain Free   Lucid
Satisfied   Relaxed   Calm

This dual-system model (conscious / subconscious) is the cornerstone of behavioural economics. Kahneman refers to the super-fast, intuitive, emotional type of thinking as "system one", and the slower, more deliberate, rational type of thinking as "system two".

We live under the illusion that our actions and behaviours are shaped by conscious thinking, but the reality is that the emotional mind makes many of our decisions for us. We use subconscious rules of thumb to help us navigate through daily life. Mostly, these work well for us, but they can be prone to some simple and predictable errors.

Too often, organisations try to use rational information to motivate people, but information in itself doesn't lead directly to action. Rather, it leads to rational conclusions, which may or may not shape behaviour.

Emotional doesn't mean 'upset', but rather evoking any kind of emotion, such as excitement, frustration, disappointment or happiness. People experience the emotion and feel the need to do something. Telling them we think doing something is a good idea isn't enough. They need to have a really good reason to want it for themselves.

Lighting a fire of inspiration, passion or desire in someone requires an emotion

Habits are automatic behaviours we perform without consciously thinking about them, and they are a function of our emotional mind. They are prompted by other actions or environmental cues that precede them. When we repeat an action often enough, we get good at anticipating the behavioural patterns connected with it, and eventually, to reduce mental demand, these actions become a habit, leaving us with extra mental capacity for other things requiring our attention. Habits can be broken and new ones learnt, but it takes repetition and conscious effort, and for this reason, people find changing their behaviour difficult.

We have to want it enough, regardless of our state of mind

Expected effort

Expected benefits

In order to successfully change behaviour, the benefits of making a change need to outweigh the pain a person goes through when making that change. Additionally, until they have succeeded in developing a new habit, people can only anticipate how easy it will be, and that prediction will be shaped by their emotions. A person feeling inspired and in a "hot" emotional state could significantly underestimate the challenge ahead whilst their motivation is high. A short while later, in a more relaxed, calm state, the same person may feel that their goal is no longer quite as important to them.

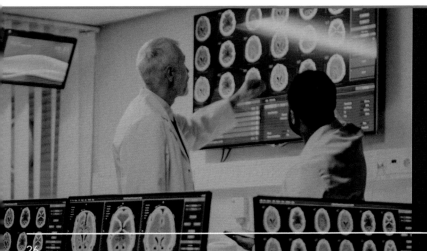

Using brain imaging equipment, scientists can observe blood flowing to different parts of the brain when we experience different states of mind. When we are excited, inspired and in an emotional state, our brains are quite literally activated differently to when we are feeling calm and rational. When we are in an emotional state, we can't quite appreciate what it feels like to be in a calm state and vice versa.

Successful and continued behaviour change requires people to still want to change, regardless of which state of mind they are in.

Xbox has the second largest following of any brand on Twitter (with 15.7 million followers as of March 2021)[4].

Did you look at the statement above and think "Okay, but what about the top one? Tell me about the top one." You may find it annoying to be left in suspense and have that puzzle unresolved. Are you now wondering if you can guess which is number one? It's likely that knowing Twitter's most popular brand account will mean nothing to you, and you will instantly forget it even when you find out, but you still want to know, right? The answer is overleaf on page 28.

Humans are naturally curious. It's one of our best characteristics and key to social cohesion and our natural inventiveness. We are endlessly curious about the world around us, how things fit together and what makes us and others tick. We find learning pleasurable. Not the kind of learning you do sitting in classrooms and revising for exams, but real intrinsic, curiosity-led learning.

DID YOU KNOW?

INTERESTING FACT

There has never been anything remotely interesting shared in a "Did you know" statement.

The subtext of all "Did you know?" statements is, "It won't be anything memorable. It's just we find it mildly interesting and we lack imagination."

Knowing people have a curiosity instinct has led lazy marketers and poor content writers to hit us with an endless stream of instantly forgettable "Did you know?" statements, framed to make the facts in them sound more interesting than they actually are. No one shares meaningful information like this in real life.

If what you have to share with us is genuinely brilliant and fascinating, then tell us all about it in full colour and emotional richness.

tell them your story

From the previous page...
Playstation is number one with
21.3 million followers (March 2021)[5].

Storytelling Masterclass

British Airways broadcast a special extended-length TV commercial in 2011 called "The Aviators". Created by the agency Bartle Bogle Hegarty and set to a specially commissioned soundtrack by Helen Jane Long, it's possibly the best example of a brand telling a story about who they are. The script is breathtakingly good and it's definitely worth 90 seconds of your day to watch.

Google: "British Airways The Aviators"
– and turn the volume up!

Look through the photograph gallery on your phone and stop at one that makes you smile to yourself. What's the story behind the picture? Imagine someone is there with you, they ask you why you are smiling into your phone and you tell them the story. Where do you start? How do you set the scene? What were the memorable moments?

Storytelling is the act of adding emotion and context to information. It's a part of our social instinct and developed as a survival mechanism to bond us together, help us collaborate and warn each other of dangers. We have been sharing stories for tens of thousands of years, far longer than we have been able to write things down.

The way we share emotional stories is more resonant and appealing to the listener than making a statement or simply relaying facts. It turns out we are terrible at remembering facts on their own, and instead recall information far more readily if we learnt it with additional emotional context.

As referred to on page 24, we operate with two types of thinking, emotional (subconscious) and rational (conscious). The emotional mind simply isn't built to comprehend rational facts and their logical implications - but it just loves a good story.

Many of us have read fiction from a young age. News programmes follow a story-based narrative. We universally like movies. If we get interrupted mid-story, like a cliff-hanger at the end of an episode in a TV series, it frustrates us. We want to know how things work out.

You have a story to tell. Your organisation has a story to tell. Your story is who you are, what you stand for, how you started, how you grew. It's where you are going, how you want to change the lives of your customers and what it means to you to be part of that.

Your customers have a story too. It's the story they tell themselves (and others) about who they are and what is important to them. They are drawn to brands, products and experiences that fit best with that personal narrative.

Can you tell better stories about your product or service? And how can you align your story with that of your customers?

Would real people have a conversation like that?

To tell good stories, you need to use good words.

"How was your weekend?"

When friends talk and share stories they use ordinary language - 'cup of tea' language, the words you'd expect to hear if you overheard two friends sitting in a café chatting about their weekend. It's free of jargon and acronyms. It's vivid, emotional and includes how they felt, why they were surprised, afraid or delighted. It's told from a very human perspective.

When you talk to your friends, what kind of daily trivia do you share? What do you find most interesting about each others' stories? What kind of language do you use?

Now check your service language. Imagine you are a customer and read your printed literature, call your customer service centre, speak to a member of the sales team, pour over your website and read the backlog of posts on social channels. Are you storytelling? Are you using cup of tea language? Would real people have a conversation like that?

"The John Lewis Christmas ad is out!"

There are a number of occasions on the calendar that hark the arrival of Christmas, a string of Christmas firsts if you like, and in the UK, you really know Christmas is on its way when the seasonal John Lewis commercial is released. It's an annual event only about 10 years in the making, but it's become a British tradition already.

Usually extended in duration, each one has been a marvel in mini-storytelling. These hyper-emotional stories, with their stripped-down acoustic soundtracks, have given us Buster the Boxer dog pining for a bounce on the new trampoline, the young girl connecting with the lonely Man on the Moon, the hare waking the bear from hibernation to experience Christmas, the Snowman looking for the perfect gift for Mrs Snowman, Monty the lonely penguin who wanted a girlfriend penguin, and Moz, the monster under the bed.

To keep up with the competition, other brands, such as Marks and Spencer and Sainsbury's have produced their own rival Christmas commercials. It's an "emotion-off" if you like, a battle for who can pull the heart-strings the hardest. In fact, the stories are so far removed from the normal look and feel of the brands behind them that it's become a game for viewers to try to guess which company made the advert before they tell us at the end.

Then while Christmas dinner is sending us all into a collective national afternoon nap, the next wave of exposure to hyper-emotional selling begins, this time for summer holidays. TUI, First Holidays, Virgin, British Airways and others expose us to viscerally appealing representations of perfect holidays; time with family, happy and well behaved children, blue skies, white sandy beaches, beautiful bikini bodies, spa treatments, empty pools, cuisine to die for…

Humans are emotionally driven decision makers. We like to think we pick and choose our way through life logically and rationally, but, in truth, we are steered by complex and subconscious emotional shortcuts and all of these commercials have something in common - they all appeal directly to our emotions. Not a single reference to anything rational. No numbers anywhere. No logic. Watch a few and see if you can spot the emotional ingredients and levers being pulled.

Imagine your service or product was to be presented in the same way as one of these television commercials. It would be stripped of all rationality and turned into a story that would grip the heart and senses in one go. Imagine that was your brief, to present your product or service as if it were the most incredible, emotionally resonant experience. How would you do it? What would the plot line be? Which emotions would you want your audience to feel?

Which emotions would you want your audience to feel?

Somehow, we get a sense of what they are feeling

It's the Olympic final of the Men's Eight in rowing. The national team are in the line-up with a chance of a medal. You're on the edge of your seat. The race is over 2,000m and will only last about five minutes, but it's agonisingly long. You're willing them on, shouting at the TV… and… you're rowing too!

Well sort of. You're bobbing forwards and backwards on your sofa like a goof, in rhythm with the rowers on the screen, unaware you're even doing it and somehow feeling that you're contributing something of value to the outcome of the race!

The football team you support are playing a key game in a championship. It's a high-stakes game. The other team are a goal in the lead and there's only 10 minutes left to go. The ball is crossed in high towards the goal. The players jump to head it. You do too… from the comfort of your lounge at home.

You watch a small child running along the pavement trip and fall. They land awkwardly on one side. You draw a sharp intake of breath and hold your hand over your opposite arm. That must have hurt.

Why is it that we behave in this way, as if to instinctively and instantly mimic the actions of another person? We don't just act like they do, somehow, we also get a sense of what they are feeling as well.

Our brains are wired with a special functionality that helps us understand the intentions and actions of other people and feel greater empathy for them. It's driven by mirror neurons that fire in response to watching someone do something action-oriented, like grab a door handle, press a button, row a boat, head a ball or fall over. Scientists have found that when we observe a distinct action taken by another person, the same parts of our minds are activated as if we were performing the action ourselves[6].

Think of an advert where you see someone step into a luxuriously warm bubble bath, or take a bite from an ice-lolly, bounce onto a brand new sofa, swim in the hotel pool on holiday, or pull open the ring-pull on a can of coke… It's a powerful technique.

We don't even need to watch it happen in real life for this effect to work. You can visualise it through hearing a vivid narrative of the action in question. If you can help your customers imagine vividly, in an action-based way, what it will feel like to use your product or service, then they won't just hear about it, but will get to "actually experience" it.

Add even more impact to your stories by including references to sensory experiences that are unique. There are some experiences we have that are so distinctive they can't be anything else. Imagine for a moment it's a cold day outside. You walk to a window to look out and you press the palm of your hand against the cold glass. That touch sensation is unique.

Standing at the water's edge on a beach with your feet in the sand. Holding a mug of hot tea (okay, the drink itself may not be unique, but the sensation of holding a mug containing a hot drink is a distinct touch experience). Hearing the happy sounds of young children running around a school playground. Holding a pack of cards in your hand. Hearing the announcements in the departure hall of a railway station. Hearing the muffled chatter of an audience waiting for a play to start.

Many stores have a signature scent, created uniquely for them, and as you walk in, you are grounded by the familiar smell. Lush, the handmade cosmetic retailer, has such a strong and distinctive signature scent you can tell you are near one of their stores while you are still down the street!

Can you refer to a signature sensory experience in the stories you share?

Even better,
can you create
a new one
with your
products?

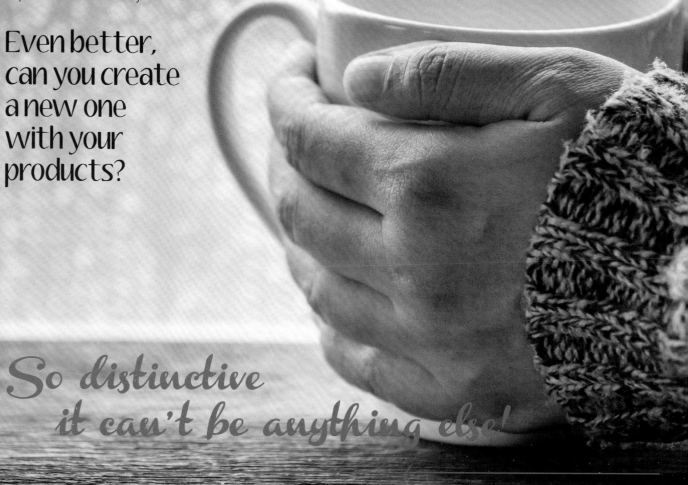

So distinctive
it can't be anything else!

66 I wish I'd bought one of these sooner. **99**

66 Wow! The finish on this is such high quality. **99**

66 The woman I spoke to on the phone was really friendly and it's all sorted now. **99**

66 It was so much easier than I thought it would be. **99**

Do you ever hear yourself saying soundbites and snippets like this about services and brands you experience?

Companies usually want feedback from customers to help them improve their services and to acknowledge staff who are doing great work. You'll see many ways different companies try to get this feedback, including adding web addresses on the bottom of receipts, customer comments cards, and buttons you can tap to indicate your level of satisfaction. Some run prize draws or offer gift vouchers as an incentive to get more people to take the time to share their opinions.

Transparency systems are used by the likes of Uber, Google, Amazon and TripAdvisor. They work on the principle that public reviews are highly trusted and keep vendors and suppliers accountable and focused on delivering great experiences to customers.

Publishing testimonials you receive from delighted customers is a great way to explain to others what to expect from you.

 Reviews (465)

Clue: lots of people said it was great!

The thing is, when people write feedback, they tend to do it very rationally. The act of thinking about a recent experience and turning it into written feedback uses the slower, more deliberate cognitive part of our minds. In contrast, conversational soundbites are usually much more 'everyday' in their language, more spontaneously given without overthinking, and more emotional in their content.

These are "accidental testimonials". They aren't offered as formal feedback, more an off-the-cuff compliment, and because it's spontaneous, it's honest, and that's valuable.

Next time you hear someone casually describe their experience or compliment a member of your team with a short throwaway comment, ask them if they mind if you write down what they just said, so you can share it as a soundbite testimonial with others.

That's right, YOU write it down, not them - exactly how they said it, and the shorter, the better.

They may say no to you sharing what they said, or they may say yes but wish to stay anonymous, but if you ask enough people you'll quickly acquire a large bank of great soundbites you can share to inspire others.

Furthermore, the very act of paying attention to the casual things customers say will be a valuable exercise in itself.

No, you write it down!
(exactly how you heard it)

66 She hasn't stopped talking about it! 99

66 I'm looking forward to coming back next week. 99

Note: All testimonials are sacred! Accidental or not. Don't mess with them. Don't change them. Don't try to improve them - we can usually tell. Just share them exactly how they were given.

The gap between our two types of thinking (rational and emotional) also shows up when we try to describe experiences and emotions using words.

Have you ever read a piece of poetry or heard a song lyric which beautifully captured a feeling you've experienced, that you'd never have been able to adequately put into words yourself?

It's so difficult because our use of words and language is mainly a conscious, rational activity, while in contrast, the feelings and emotions we want to describe are subconscious, emotional experiences. We simply struggle to find words that are adequate enough to describe the richness and nuance of emotions.

There are some wonderful examples from non-English languages, where they have words for emotions and experiences we are all familiar with. Some examples:

Hygge (🔊 hoo-ga) - This well-known Danish word describes that pleasant, genial feeling of being warm and cozy indoors in winter.

Iktsuarpok (🔊 eek-soow-uhr-pohk) - This Inuit word describes the irresistible urge we have to keep looking out of the window when we are expecting a visitor to arrive. (A modern version of this is checking your phone every few minutes if you are expecting a message!)

Pena Ajena (🔊 pain-a a-hina) - A Spanish term to describe the acute embarrassment we feel on behalf of other people, such as when a singer drops a bad note in a performance, or someone falls over in public.

Gjensynsglede (🔊 en-sen-glee-rah) - Norwegians have a word for the joy you feel when you meet up with someone you haven't seen in ages.

Here are some other experiences we should have words for:

□ The growing sense of alarm you feel when your mobile phone battery has less than 5% charge remaining.

□ The disappointment you feel when something turns out not to be as good as advertised, like a holiday destination, a Tinder date or an apartment you have viewed.

□ The joy of waking up early and realising you can still have two more hours of sleep before the alarm goes off.

□ The pleasant feeling you get at the end of the Saturday of a Bank Holiday weekend as you contemplate that you still have two more days off work.

□ The moment you take off uncomfortable high-heeled shoes and walk on plush carpet.

□ In a restaurant, when you have been so busy chatting with your friends you haven't yet looked at the menu, and the waiter comes back to see if you are ready to order… for the third time.

□ In the same restaurant, that panicky feeling you get when your friends start ordering their food and you still have no idea what you want.

What other emotions do we need words for?

The "cocktail party effect" is a phenomenon we've all experienced[7]. Imagine you're in a busy, noisy room full of people, with many conversations going on, such as at a bar or cocktail party. You're deep in conversation with someone and suddenly, through all the noise, you hear someone else nearby utter your name. In that moment, your attention is pulled out of the conversation you're in, and directed instead to the person you just heard mention your name. Suddenly you want to know what they want or what they were saying. That's the cocktail party effect.

It happens because while our conscious attention is focused on the conversation we're in, our senses are still subconsciously drawing in information from all around us, including peripheral sounds. There are some sounds we are conditioned to react to, sounds that instantly demand priority for our attention, and one of them is the sound of someone saying our name.

It demonstrates how important names are to us. After all, we've been responding to people calling us by our name for longer than we can remember. It's deeply embedded conditioning.

'Tartle' is a great word from Scotland, which describes that slightly panicky feeling you get when you are about to introduce someone and you can't remember their name! You'll know this feeling because we've all been there and it's great that there's a word for it.

Having someone take the effort to remember your name makes you feel good, makes you instinctively like them more and strengthens the social bond between you both. On the other hand, having someone forget your name subconsciously weakens that connection. This is why we feel an excruciating moment of panic when we are the person who forgets.

Calling your customers by name makes them feel more special. It makes your interaction with them feel more human and more individual. Without overdoing it (we all know what it feels like when telemarketers overuse our name), how can you create that personal touch when you connect with customers?

What are your early memories of technology? Did you have a wireless analogue radio, a VHS video player or Sony Walkman? Which toys were your childhood favourites? What was the first movie you saw in a cinema? What was the first record you ever bought? What was your school uniform like? What did you do during the school holidays? Where were you living ten years ago? Twenty years ago?

Ask your friends, family or work colleagues any of the above and you'll find it triggers a conversation punctured with stories, wistful laughter and moments of intense nostalgia. You get that feeling that life was more simple then. Things were "somehow better in those days".

nostalgia

Pronunciation: /nɒˈstaldʒə

noun: a sentimental longing for the past

Nostalgia comes from two Greek words that essentially mean "homecoming pain", but it's less about a specific place, and more of a general feeling about a time in our lives. While nostalgia may seem to be a negative experience, scientists believe it serves a positive function[8]. People who experience naturally frequent moments of nostalgia report greater wellbeing and more optimism about the future. It appears to serve as a way of providing a sense of continuity in our lives, a better connection with others and more gratitude for things we have now.

It's a rose-tinted illusion though. In those nostalgic moments we airbrush out all the negative feelings and the daily frustrations we experienced in the past, and instead gloss over the memory with a positive emotion. Even sad times become bitter-sweet. Because it's in the past, we also know how things turned out, so memories have a cosy certainty to them, unlike the daily things we struggle with today.

The biggest nostalgia triggers come from smells (a favourite meal your mother made you when you were a child, the perfume worn by your first love), and sounds (like the tunes you and your friends listened to one carefree summer). Smells and sounds bypass the thinking brain and go straight to the emotional centre, where it quickly changes our emotional state.

For a dose of nostalgia, visit thenostalgiamachine.com, choose a year and be entertained by that year's greatest hits.

You don't even have to have lived through an era yourself to feel nostalgia for it. Thanks to the rich array of vivid multi-media stories, movies and advertising, it's possible to still experience nostalgia for something we haven't personally experienced before.

If your product or service (or your marketing) can somehow connect customers with their former selves, it will evoke a strong positive emotion in them and contribute to a feeling of optimism. Remember too, your customers' experience now could become part of a nostalgic memory for their future selves…

What does it mean in human terms?

Have you ever prepared some communications or a press release about how much you are investing in a new service or product? £8 million, £250,000…? What does £8 million look like as a pile of cash? In £20 notes, it's about a bathtub full. Impressive? Not really. What does that mean in human terms? Do you talk about what your investment will feel like in changing the outcomes and quality of life for your customers?

In the same way as described in earlier pages, we struggle to connect to big numbers. To make sense of a large amount of money, people have to anchor it against a number they are familiar with, like their annual wage or the value of their house. This can make a figure like £8 million seem like a huge amount of money, but doesn't really make us feel the impact of how far that money will stretch.

Think of charities that need millions of pounds each year to continue their valuable work. Are you more compelled to donate if you think your hard-earned contribution will be added to the vast bucket of money needed just to maintain "business as usual" or would you feel more compelled to donate if they told you that your contribution would pay for "a mosquito net", "support for a bereaved person" or "a hot meal for a homeless person"? As soon as the number becomes easier to visualise, it has more emotional impact, and the desire to contribute becomes stronger.

In a television nature series about the animals on the plains of Africa:

Week 1 is about the Impala antelope, about the life and survival of this herd animal. The narrator focuses on a young female and her calf, about the vulnerability of the youngster, especially when it gets separated a short distance from the rest of the herd. A big cat stalks the baby. We lean towards the television, on the edge of our seats. "Run little one, don't let the big bad cat get you."

Week 2 is about the big cats. The narrator tells us about a lioness and her litter of lion cubs and we watch them tumble and play. The mother is hungry and weak. She needs to catch some food to stay strong and to provide for her babies. She doesn't want to leave them because they are still vulnerable, but she has no choice. If she doesn't eat they will all starve. The lion sees a small antelope separated from the herd. It won't feed her and her cubs for long but it'll give them a chance. We lean towards the television, on the edge of our seats… "Run mamma, catch some food and feed your babies!"

It's the same story, but the way the narrative is set up for us determines who we care about the most. It's an example of how we become emotionally invested in one side of a scenario based on how it's told.

How a story is framed matters. It determines who or what we become emotionally invested in.

Who do you want to win?

We are much more concerned with what happens within our own lives, the lives of our families and our closest friends. We care much less about the outcomes others experience, especially strangers. That doesn't mean we don't care about others at all, but that we are our own priority. Our experience of the world is from our own perspective. We are all right at the centre of our own universes.

When you talk about your service, do you talk in terms of your organisational goals rather than the goals of your customers? For example, "Our organisation aims to get more people active." "We need to stop people without life-threatening conditions from turning up at A&E." "Missed appointments cost the taxpayer money." How can you reframe what you say so that it is more about the customer?

It's about what they want, not what you want. What does your product or service mean to them?

If you are committed to putting customers first, how do you find out what they want? Ask them, "What one thing would make your life easier?" "What would rock your world?"

Your customer is here

Centre of the Universe

Arrive happy!

The Boeing 787 Dreamliner has revolutionised air travel. The majority of the fuselage and wings on a 787 is made from composite materials, making it lighter and more efficient with a longer flying range. It's therefore cheaper to operate and more flexible, because it can travel more routes. This is the headline stuff you hear about the Dreamliner.

On a tour of the Boeing Experience at the Everett site in Seattle, Washington, the guide explains, "Oh the Dreamliner is great! You'll see it doesn't need a protective green coating on it while we build it. It's because it's composite, so it doesn't rust. That also means when you fly in a Dreamliner, they don't have to take the moisture out of the cabin air [which could rust a regular metal frame], so you sleep better, you feel better and you arrive at your destination feeling much better."

Why don't we hear that information? Tell us first how much it improves our flying experience and then tell us it's cheaper for the airline to operate!

Talking about your service in general terms misses an opportunity to connect with customers and make them feel special.

For example, delivering a learn-to-swim programme that teaches 3,000 children a year to swim sounds impressive, but a parent is only interested in their own child. If you say "We have the best teachers at our pool, who are personally committed to teaching your child to be a confident swimmer before your next holiday", it sounds much more compelling.

Nice touch!

Thomson Holidays, which was one of the UK's biggest travel companies, used to send customers a book about their holidays in advance of their departure. It wasn't just a travel guide about their destination, but a completely personalised book about their actual holiday.

About 40 pages, stitch-bound and A6 in size, it was a compilation of everything customers could need or want to know about their holiday: their hotel, their destination, suggestions for days out, typical weather for the time of year, and flight, airport and transfers information. Flight tickets and luggage labels could be found at the back of the book.

It was as if someone at Thomson HQ had personally sat down and researched each of their customers' holidays and then hand made a unique little book, with love, for each of them.

emotion — inspiration

To get from information to inspiration, you need to add emotion.

To make your service connect with a customer, it has to address at least one of their emotional needs. An emotional need is a sponsoring thought, a driver. It's their source of motivation.

For example, a person doesn't necessarily have a need to take a train journey, but they may really want to spend time with someone at their destination.

A person may not have the need to buy a new shirt, but they may find they like how they look when they try it on in a fitting room, which makes them feel good about themselves.

An anxious parent may choose to take their child to the Emergency Department because they want immediate reassurance that it's nothing serious.

To find the emotional need, just keep asking "why?" Why would they do that? Why would they want that? What difference would that make to them? What problem would it solve?

Ask your customers what difference your product or service makes in their lives. You may be surprised at what you uncover.

Why?

"I've come to really like frozen yoghurt. There's something so human about taking something great and ruining it a little so you can have more of it."

Michael (The Good Place, S1, E6)

In Netflix's "The Good Place", Ted Danson plays Michael, an angel-like architect who has designed the afterlife where the best people get to go when they die. He is constantly perplexed by the human condition, and due to demand, has filled the neighbourhood with frozen yoghurt outlets.

If humans were entirely rational, we would always make decisions that were in our best interests. Given an array of options, and with limitless capacity for making detailed comparisons, rational humans would take out pensions at the first opportunity, save money where the interest rates gave the best returns, only buy things they needed to use, switch energy suppliers regularly to get the best deals and complete college assignments early.

REAL humans, on the other hand, are sub-optimal decision-makers. Especially decisions that are complex, involving many factors and where the outcome of that decision is a long time off. We don't have the mental capacity to think our way logically through every option and outcome, so we apply heuristics and biases, which makes our lives much easier, but can leave us a little error-prone. We would barely admit to how we figure stuff out, if we even knew how we did it.

Imagine someone built a supercomputer that could tell you every decision and every action you need to take to lead the longest, healthiest, wealthiest life (or whatever you think success looks like).

All you would need to do is put your life's goal into the machine and it will calculate the optimal path for you... what to eat for lunch, what time to go to bed, what to wear, which course to enrol on, which street to buy your house in, who to marry...

Did you have an allergic reaction to the paragraph above? It's possible such a computer could exist, if not now, soon. If you could get one, would you use it? If you used it, would you act on what it said, or would you argue back?

Or do you prefer to stumble your way

heart-first

through life like every other human?

Our cognitive brainpower is a limited resource. While the unconscious, emotional part of our brains seems to have unlimited processing ability, the rational part is prone to getting depleted.

Think of your rational mind a bit like a mobile phone. It needs recharging every night, which it does as you sleep. But your rational brain isn't like any modern mobile phone battery, it's more like that old phone you used to have a few years ago, where even if you start the day 100% charged, you're still depleted by mid-afternoon.

Once you have exhausted the critical, rational, thinking part of your mind, you're left a bit like an unsupervised toddler at the end of the day, prone to feeling more emotional, more vulnerable and more dissatisfied... more susceptible to evening TV advertising selling you products that put it all right!

These are some factors that speed up the depletion of our cognitive capacity (like leaving an old mobile phone out in the open on a freezing cold day!)

Cognitive effort

A day of focused mental work activity and decision-making will drain our battery faster than a relaxing weekend day. The harder we work and the more we have to concentrate, the faster the drain. If you have to make important decisions in your work (or life), you are better to get them out of the way earlier in the day while you still have some rational capacity to provide checks and balances to what your emotional mind will choose for you.

Emotional state

Being in any kind of emotional state will burn through your cognitive capacity faster than if you were feeling calm. Emotional doesn't just mean upset, but any state - angry, frustrated, sad, excited...

Complexity

Some problems are just more complex than others. If the implications and factors you need to consider are multiplied, your mental battery will drain faster.

Novelty

When everything is new around you and you have to learn how to do something for the first time it consumes more cognitive power. It's why you're exhausted at the end of the day when you start a brand-new job. Even if you don't think you achieved much, you still had to find the bathroom, the kitchen and how to get back into the building after lunch.

Willpower

Willpower takes mental effort. Think you are doing yourself a favour by refusing a mid-morning treat in the coffee break at the conference? People who have to exert a lot of willpower become more drained later in the day. It's why people often overconsume high-sugar and high-fat food at night when they have been more disciplined in the day. Resisting that conference cookie may have just cost you your attention in the 4-5pm presentation.

Distraction

Switching gear all day long consumes additional brain power. This includes going to non-stop meetings all day long on different topics, or stopping and starting on your work because the demands of your email keep taking your attention. It's a good reason to schedule specific time to spend on email and to minimise the number of meetings you attend.

You end up a bit like an unsupervised toddler at the end of the day

- Do you lead with facts rather than emotions? Are you basing your messages on a rational argument rather than an emotional one? Do you think it will make people feel something? If not, take another look.

- Many communications are based on answering the second question first: how much, how often... The first question should always be "why would you want it so much?" "What difference would it make to your life?" Have you got your questions in the right order? Are you asking your customers the right questions first?

- Do you use a lot of numbers in your messages? And are you compounding the numbers by combining them, such as using lots of statistics and percentages together? Try to eliminate or reduce the numbers in your message.

- Is there a better way you could help customers to visualise any numbers that you do need to use? Can you create a strong mental image? Can you use infographics to help the numbers tell a story?.

- Are you using great images to augment your marketing and content? A great image can influence the emotional state of a customer and help them to feel more inspired.

- What are your Key Performance Indicators? Do you broadcast them as news when you reach them? Do you promote your investments as news? "We built a £6 million new swimming pool". If you find that you do, can you emphasise how much your news will change the lives of your customers for the better?

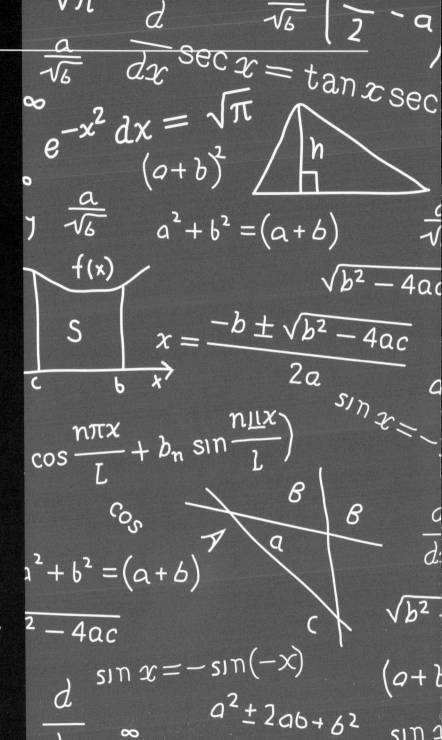

■ Do you try to persuade customers to access your service or buy your product based on what you want and your organisation's objectives? Or do you entirely focus on their needs and wants? Make it about the customer every time. (Side note: take time to find out from customers what they want and need the most.)

■ Do you use rhetorical "Did you know?" questions? Do you believe they really evoke curiosity in people? While humans are curious by nature, "Did you know?" statements never live up to expectation. If it's an insight worth sharing, just share it.

■ Will your customers be in an emotional state at any point when they use your service? For example, are they excited, happy, sad, tired, anxious or hungry at any point? Is the trigger for customers using your service linked to their emotional state? Is there a step in your customer journey they will feel a particular emotional high or low?

■ Take a look at all the ways in which you communicate with customers. In print, social media, word of mouth, press releases, on the telephone, in person… Check your language – is it 'cup of tea' language? Would you expect to hear two people having a real conversation like that?

■ Do you have any great stories you can share, such as testimonials from delighted customers? Do you have any case studies and examples of how real people tackled their problems, changed their course and how your service or product made a big difference in their lives?

■ When your customers give you a short conversational soundbite or compliment, are you writing it down and asking if you can tell other people what they have said? Accidental testimonials are particularly powerful because they are short and authentic.

- What is your story? Your reason for being? What is the history about why you are who you are? Is it a consistent message, and are you sharing it through every channel you have available?

- Can you use more emotional words when you describe your product or service? Use inspiring words that evoke feelings.

- Is your service memorable? Does your key message stand out? Will people remember receiving your letter, seeing your poster, hearing your advert, meeting your staff, visiting your facility? Will they think about you when you most want them to?

- Are you using your customers' names? Addressing them by name makes them feel important and heard. We are used to responding to our names, and if you demonstrate to customers you took the effort to remember theirs, it will make them feel good.

- Can you make your service more personal to make customers feel more special and important? How can you go above-and-beyond to make sure their experience is a good one?

- Can you create your own distinctive sensory experience? Such as a signature scent or a specific hand-feel of your product.

- Can you evoke a feeling of nostalgia for customers? Nostalgia is a powerful emotion, and its rose-tinted glow will be cast over your product or service too.

Short term

People prefer things they can have now over things they can have in the future

"Investment behaviour" describes our behaviour when we are working for something in the future. It's when we are prepared to sacrifice something now, such as time, money or effort, in exchange for benefits we can have in the future. For example, putting money in a pension, for the benefit of a more comfortable retirement (which may still be several decades away), rather than enjoying the money now, is obvious investment behaviour.

Less obvious investment behaviours include building a career, studying for a degree, working on a DIY project at home. In investment behaviour, we offset the pleasure we could have now to make things better in the future. The word cloud below describes aspects of investment behaviour.

careful

responsible protect

boring risk averse

investment

future planned

return hard work

long-term interest

safe

"Experience behaviour" is the opposite to investment behaviour and is about the here and now. Experience behaviour is enjoying immediate benefits with disregard for its future cost. Great examples of experience behaviour can be seen when we are on holiday. We may buy an ice cream, go out for dinner, drink an extra cocktail or glass of wine, go for a day out, or just sit by the pool and read a book, because we can and purely for the joy of it.

Experience behaviour is spending our resources on something we want now, even at the expense of something we would far prefer to have in the future. Anyone who has ever struggled to save up for something they really want, and instead spent money on momentary treats will know this effect. This word cloud describes experience behaviour.

Hint: We have an instinctive preference for these →

thrill exciting
immediate indulgent
short-term rewarding
experience
here and now great
fun enjoyable
memorable spontaneous

We flip-flop between the two modes. No-one remains permanently in one, although we all know people who spend more time in one mode or other. A person who is always in investment mode will probably be told by friends to "live a little". A person who is always in experience mode will probably be told by friends to be more cautious and start "saving for a rainy day".

We experience tension when we mix up the two types of behaviour. For example, if you take work away on holiday with you, your partner and your colleagues will probably tell you to stop working, put your emails away and enjoy yourself. On the other hand, if you spend all your time at work browsing social media and doing non-work-related tasks, you'll probably also be called out!

It's hardwired into us to prefer to be in experience mode. We have an instinctive preference for things we can have right now over the things we can have in the future. You may also have noticed that as well as being about time, the words in the 'investment' cloud are more rational and the words in the 'experience' cloud are more emotional, another reason we are drawn to them.

Do your products or services focus on making people's lives better in the future? If so, how do you describe them? Do you talk in terms of the investment, the future benefits? Or can you find a few things they are going to love about them right now? Can you make them and the way you talk about them more experiential?

SALE
ITALIAN STYLE
£24 per month
was £1,779

NOW £864

3 YEARS
INTEREST FREE
CREDIT

Typical
0%
APR

BUY NOW PAY LATER

Imagine you go shopping for a new sofa and you see one you want to buy. It's £864 in the sale, so you feel you have to act fast before the price goes up again. Let's say you can't afford to buy it outright, so you have two choices…

1) You can take out interest-free credit, have your sofa delivered in two weeks and pay £24 per month for the next 36 months.

2) You can save £24 per month and in 36 months' time go back and hope it's still there and still the same price.

For the exact same financial cost do you want it now or in three years' time? The likelihood is that it won't be available in three years but you could still be confident of finding another sofa you like. Though, with option two will you be disciplined enough to save your money?

Or do you think you'll find other things to spend it on in the meantime? Sofa or no sofa?

If the financial transaction is exactly the same, due to the interest-free credit offer, most of us would choose to have the sofa immediately rather than wait. In fact, the most rational of us would calculate that with the effect of inflation, it is actually cheaper (marginally) to buy the sofa on interest-free credit now. Besides, you probably just did a quick mental redecorating of your lounge and know exactly where you'll put it and what accessories you'll buy to go with it!

Buy now pay later fits with our instinctive preference to have things sooner rather than later. It's not just financial, it's also how we approach course assignments, our health, the environment… anything where we experience a tension between now and later.

saving for a healthier future

Children's Trust Funds

Giving your child a healthy head start

saving for a healthier future

Pension Schemes

Plan for a healthy retirement

saving for a healthier future

Active Bonds & ISAs

Save for the important things in life

lifestyle bank

Encouraging people to change their behaviour now for a long-term gain is similar to selling a savings account, and the further away from today that the benefits can be realised, the harder it becomes to "sell" the product. Long-term good health is an incredibly good thing to have, but so is a pension, and how many people enjoy saving up for those?

The underlying savings-style message is, "do something today that you would prefer not to, do it regularly from now on, and at some point in the far future, you may enjoy the benefit."

Notice the use of the word "may" in the line above. Many of the benefits we talk about aren't guaranteed. We tell people that if they walk 10,000 steps a day, they are likely to live longer, and we tell people that eating more fruit and vegetables will help to prevent them from having a heart attack, but there are no certainties of the benefits. Despite their efforts, they may still experience a heart attack and they may still die young.

If these were actual financial products, we wouldn't put our money anywhere near them!

lifestyle bank

Terms & Conditions
☐ 20 years' notice required
☐ regular pay-in required
☐ return not guaranteed

If these were actual financial products we were selling, we would have to be far more explicit about the small print so that people knew that there was a likelihood they wouldn't get the benefit they were hoping for at the end.

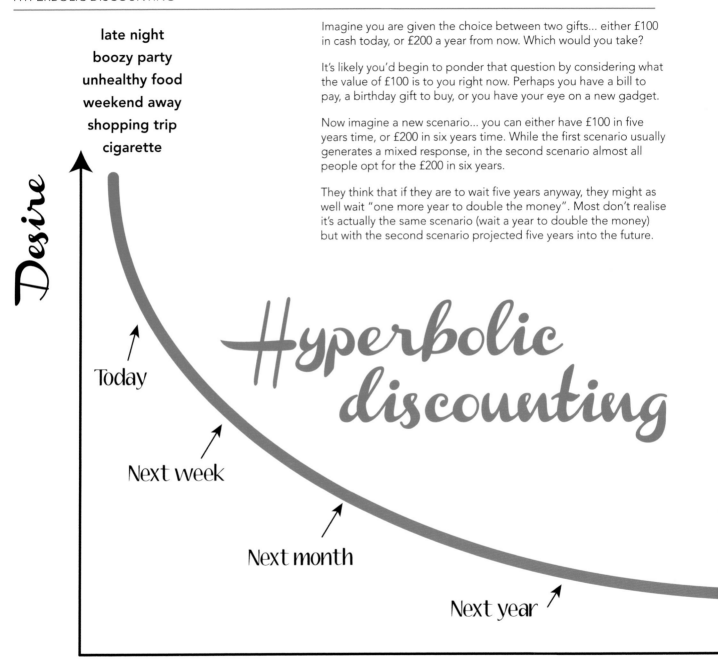

late night
boozy party
unhealthy food
weekend away
shopping trip
cigarette

Desire

Today

Next week

Next month

Next year

Hyperbolic discounting

Imagine you are given the choice between two gifts... either £100 in cash today, or £200 a year from now. Which would you take?

It's likely you'd begin to ponder that question by considering what the value of £100 is to you right now. Perhaps you have a bill to pay, a birthday gift to buy, or you have your eye on a new gadget.

Now imagine a new scenario... you can either have £100 in five years time, or £200 in six years time. While the first scenario usually generates a mixed response, in the second scenario almost all people opt for the £200 in six years.

They think that if they are to wait five years anyway, they might as well wait "one more year to double the money". Most don't realise it's actually the same scenario (wait a year to double the money) but with the second scenario projected five years into the future.

In the first scenario, 'today' is on the table, and that makes it more attractive.

The reason behind this is a bias called the "hyperbolic discount"[9]. It's connected to how we understand time and value. When time is involved, we don't compare things directly to make a decision. Instead, we instinctively reduce the value of things we have to wait for before we compare them to things we can have today.

Future benefits incur a value penalty.

This means a £10 item we can have now is worth more to us than the same £10 item we can have in a months' time. The shopping trip we can have this weekend is worth more to us than keeping the same money in our savings account for a couple of decades. The cigarette we can have now, the high-calorie takeaway, or the extra alcohol units are worth more now than the good health we can experience in the future…

We could play with different hypothetical amounts of cash, and different durations of time and we would find that there comes a cross-over point where we will switch our decision between the smaller or larger amount.

The amount by which we are prepared to accept a lower return for the benefit of having it immediately is the 'discount'. It shows we place an unseen additional value on having something now rather than having to wait for it.

If the main benefits customers will get from using your product or service is a little way off yet, or a long way, are there any shorter, more immediate benefits you can talk about? It's fine to talk about long-term benefits, just don't make them the headline.

Also, if customers are more instinctively drawn towards experience behaviour, what great short-term emotional experience can they have of your service or product right now?

We have a greater desire for things if we can have them now

...so, can you bring forward the perceived befefits of your product or service?

5 years 10 years

6 years 20 years

sustainable future
long-term good health
healthy future finances

Time

You receive a notice to say the road outside your workplace is going to be closed for resurfacing in a couple of weeks' time. It will be closed for four days and you'll need to find somewhere else to park your car. You think to yourself it'll be an inconvenience, but the road is in a bad state, and anyway, it's a few weeks off yet. You'll worry about it when it happens.

Even up until a couple of days before the road closure it's "that thing that's happening soon". Then the day arrives and it's total chaos! Between all the traffic diversions and the extra people trying to park on nearby side streets, you end up late for your first meeting and spend the rest of the day playing catch-up. Your journey home takes 15 minutes longer than planned too. The next three days feel like forever!

A week later, you admire the smooth new tarmac and have forgotten already what the disruption felt like just a few days earlier. It feels like weeks ago already.

Time distortion is one of the main challenges we face when it comes to changing behaviour. Humans have a poor grasp of the passage of time, and how our emotions, motivations, intentions and memory changes, even from moment to moment. You will have experienced the phenomenon where an event in the far past feels very recent and when a recent event feels like a much longer time ago. Have you booked a future trip or an event that felt like it was so far away it would never arrive? Then suddenly, it's here, and just as quickly, it's a long-distant memory.

Imagine you have to wait 24 hours for something you really want. You'll get it this time tomorrow. Now imagine it's four weeks from now and your future self has to wait a day for something too. Most people find the gap between now and tomorrow feels longer than the gap between 28 and 29 days from now.

It's because we think of time in a hyperbolic way, rather than in a linear way. We don't see time, instead we experience it, and our experience is affected by things like our attention and our emotions. Our experience is also a product of 'now' – always based on and judged from where we are right now.

It's only for 4 days...

How does time show up in your product or service?

- Are you selling something that won't be experienced for a long time, like concert tickets or travel? Or something really imminent, like an emergency repair?

- Do customers have to wait for it to be delivered?

- Does it take a long time for customers to go through each step of your service, or is it a simple, one-off thing?

- Do they have to wait to get started, referred, or approved?

- Are you relying on a third party for their contribution?

- Will customers wish their experience would last longer (like a relaxing spa treatment), or shorter (time sitting in the dentist chair)?

- Do customers get the benefit of their purchase or investment now? Or a really long time from now?

- Do customers have to collect items over time, or work their way through levels?

- Does waiting make it a better experience, like a great wine, or a beautifully cooked dinner?

- Is yours a service that creates anxiety and tension and deals with people when they feel vulnerable and afraid? Where dragging it out any longer would just be unkind?

- Is the next opportunity your customers will have to access your service a long time away, by which time it may be too late?

1/2 hour | **08 hours** | **01 day**

0 (start) | **01** hour | **03** days

Draw a timeline of what people will get if they access your service

What might change for customers in an hour? In a day? A week? A month? Three months? A year? 20 years? Plot the timeline of how your customers will benefit from your product or service, starting from the immediate moment, through to years from now.

Which of the benefits you have listed do you normally promote and talk to customers about the most? Are there any at the shorter, pointier end of the timeline you can highlight more?

If someone bought your product or used your service today, what benefit would they actually get today? If you can't think of any 'today benefits', take another look... The list below may give you some ideas:

☐ Having experienced something new

☐ Removal of pain

☐ Reassurance

☐ Connecting with others

☐ A few smiles

☐ Owning a cool new item

☐ Knowing how to use the above cool new item

☐ A happy child (or friend, spouse, or parent...)

☐ A look of gratitude

☐ Belly laughs

☐ Knowing that someone can help

☐ A confidence boost

☐ An energy boost

☐ Inspiration

☐ Knowing the result of something

☐ A listening ear (real indulgence)

☐ A feeling of excitement

01 month   **01** year   **05** years

01 week   **06** months   **20** years

and some more...

- [ ] A first step and a plan

- [ ] Being introduced to an idea you had never considered before

- [ ] Personal pride and satisfaction at getting started

- [ ] A better night's sleep

- [ ] The feeling of having contributed

- [ ] Having been entertained for a moment

- [ ] Learning a new skill

- [ ] A feeling of having invested in yourself

- [ ] Feeling important

- [ ] Joining the intangible 'club' of people who buy from your brand

What short term feedback can you give? While the actual physical benefits of behaviour change may be months away, you have the power to provide a really instant benefit… praise. What authentic immediate feedback and praise can you give?

Instant authentic positive feedback

You're doing brilliantly already!

You've mastered that skill really well.

"Your technique is great." "I'm so impressed with your progress." "You're picking up those skills so quickly." "You're doing brilliantly already." "If only all my clients were as determined as you."

How many of the emotional benefits you can offer are down to the personality and actions of you and your colleagues? How can you make interacting with your team a much more lovely or fun experience for customers?

What is your today product?

Spare 30 seconds?

There was a time in the past when we stood at bus stops and we were a little bit bored, even just for a few minutes. We read the bus stop advertisement poster, pretended we hadn't observed the other people waiting and idly stared up the street for what felt like a really long time. Standing on the platform waiting for a train, waiting for the pedestrian crossing to signal us to cross, waiting in the store for an available fitting room so we could try something on, in line at the supermarket checkout… all the same.

We used to have idle time, but not any more

Now that we have smartphones and ready access to mobile data, we have found a way of entertaining ourselves for even the shortest amount of time.

Waiting in line anywhere? Out come our phones. Even if the pause in our day is only 20-30 seconds, we have found we can do some digital activity in that time. We can read a text, post a tweet, check our bank balances, read a news headline, refresh our Facebook feed or add a heart to half a dozen Instagram photographs.

If we can't remember the name of an actor we've seen, or a place we've recently been, our phones can give us the answer in a matter of seconds.

We have conditioned ourselves to respond to the feeling of momentary boredom with some sort of fleeting digital activity. Most of it is nothing more than information sugar – instantly forgettable and insignificant. But we still get that little buzz of pleasure as a reward for having 'completed' a task.

Our instinct towards instant gratification is accelerating.

People live in the here and now so much they are no longer prepared to wait long to find information, resolve a situation or have a question answered.

If you want to harness this behaviour, ask yourself if there is a transaction your customers can do if they have a spare 20-30 seconds. Is there a way you can engage with them in that time? Is there a step of your customer journey they can quickly take? Can they register, sign up, make a decision, make a purchase? In what way can you meet your customers' desire to have things resolved instantaneously?

Millions of pictures are uploaded to Instagram every day. Pictures of all kinds. If you see one you like, you can add a little heart by tapping it. Great pictures can receive hundreds or thousands of "likes", especially those posted by celebrities.

There are some incredible photographs on Instagram, some where the photographer must have climbed mountains, cycled for miles, stayed out overnight, or waited a long time for the right moment. Many tell wonderful human stories, with strong messages of joy, heartache, nostalgia and relationships.

Occasionally we linger on a picture for a while but mostly we give these incredible pictures…. probably between 0.5 and 3 seconds of attention before we scroll down to see what else there is… It could be the best photograph you have ever seen and we afford it a matter of seconds before moving on, just in case there is something better to see… keep scrolling…

The problem is that you will never get to see all of the pictures. There are just too many of them. There are always more to see, if you just scroll down a little further... and as you don't know what you are going to see, it makes the reward unknown and variable. The next picture you see might just be amazing... keep scrolling…

When we experience something pleasant we get a release of dopamine, a brain chemical that causes us to feel good. Repeating the behaviour gives us more dopamine, encouraging us to seek opportunities to do it all over again. However, it's a process of diminishing returns, as the experience becomes predictable and the dopamine high decreases.

Scientists have proven that humans develop addictive behaviour faster when the reward and the dopamine releases are variable and unpredictable. This makes Instagram an immediate-term variable-dose-dopamine-producing platform.

Image sugar

It's also how Twitter works, and Facebook, and any other platform where there is more content to discover if you just scroll a little further. If you need evidence of how hardwired we are to seek out these short-term rewards, hop on a bus, tube or train, and look around you. You will not only see people looking at their smartphones, but you'll be able to observe them scrolling and scrolling.

This is one of those images mentioned on the previous page. North Wales photographer Kris Williams spent a night in the freezing cold Snowdonia mountains to capture this breathtaking image.

It might get no more than a couple of seconds of your attention on Instagram or Facebook, but take a few moments now to really appreciate it.

Kris Williams

Flickr: flickr.com/photos/jixxer

Glyder Fach, Snowdonia

Our expectations on having what we want quickly have been shaped by things we can do in sectors such as shopping, travel and entertainment. Starbucks allows you to place your coffee order ahead and jump the queue when you arrive. Open Table enables you to book a table at a restaurant while you are already on your way there. In many stores, you can buy or reserve an item online and turn up later to collect it.

Amazon spearheaded the same day delivery service, and in Seattle, where the company is headquartered, the most popular purchases when it trialled instant drone delivery were hotdogs and beer for people having summer parties.

We expect to be able to find products online 24/7, complete online transactions at times that suit us and we find it frustrating to have to wait until office hours to speak to someone if we get stuck. If customers have to wait, they may change their minds or go elsewhere.

Can you enable customers to sign-up for your services or buy your products in the moment, when they feel the most compelled, regardless of what time of day or night it is?

And in what way can you offer support instantly to customers when they need it most?

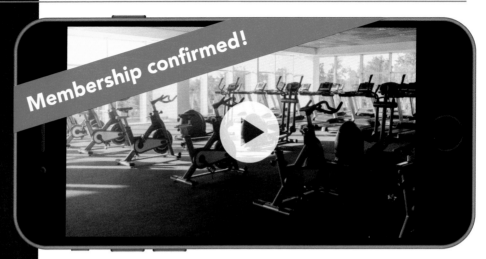

Membership confirmed!

↖ your new life

Inspiration is a strong emotion. If customers feel inspired to act, give them the facility to sign up, make a purchase or commitment while they are still in that inspired state.

Food delivery services advertise to us just as we are feeling hungry. We may find ourselves subscribing to an online fitness programme while we are feeling down about our lack of fitness. We may text for information on stopping smoking while we are frustrated we can't seem to stop on our own. We may see an advert for a product we like on television and order one for ourselves a few moments later.

Be aware that digital tools can give us a false illusion of progress. We may have signed up for an online fitness membership but not yet done a single class. We may have downloaded that app that will help us learn to speak Spanish, but we haven't yet sat down and done any focused work on it.

Once we are committed, we are more likely to follow through compared to if we let the moment of inspiration pass, so digital tools can at least get us to a point of commitment, and from there we are more likely to get started.

Digital tools can create the illusion of getting started

"A journey of a thousand miles starts with a single step"

This old proverb is used to encourage people to get started on a process that could be difficult and take a long time - taking that first step.

The thing is, in a journey of a thousand miles, it's not the first step that is the hard one. On the first step, you feel fresh, are full of optimism, you have clean socks and you just ate breakfast.

We can kid ourselves that we have cracked a new behaviour by the fact we got started, and when we experience some early success. In the same way, a person may feel excited about saving their first £5 towards an expensive purchase. We also tend to believe that regardless of the challenge that lies ahead, our motivation and enthusiasm will remain as high as it feels at the start. Of course we are going to eat a light salad for lunch every day for the next six weeks. Of course we will start all our college assignments early. Of course we will still want to do a 6am fitness class in a month's time…

People feel great about taking those first steps.

...but you have clean socks and you just ate breakfast!

It's the ones that follow that may be more difficult, because the end goal can still seem so far away, while the initial excitement of getting started begins to subside. Going back to the thousand-mile journey analogy, it's not the start that's hard, it's at mile 150, when you have blisters on your feet, you've run out of food, are tired and need a good shower – that's when it gets hard. And you're not even at a quarter of the way yet! That's when you need to be digging deep into your reserve of motivation.

Supporting your customers to get started is important, and also exciting and fun. But what's more important is how you can also support them at mile 150, and mile 362, and mile 509...

New Life

Chapter One

Relapse rates on people trying to quit smoking are stark. Only a small percentage of people actually manage to quit, and those who do typically take a number of attempts before they finally break the habit. The addictiveness of nicotine and the repeatedly rehearsed habitual behaviours surrounding smoking make it particularly hard to stop. It's been a public health priority for decades, and the number of smokers has steadily decreased, but we could still do more.

Launched in the UK in October 2012, Stoptober marked an interesting and brave shift in the way the NHS encouraged people to quit smoking. Stoptober is a month-long challenge for people to quit smoking and it's just for the month of October. What's brave and different about it is the second part of the unspoken campaign subtext.

Challenge yourself to stop just for one month

(You can always start again in November)

The bit they don't actually say

Before Stoptober, stop smoking campaigns had always been focused on the "quit for good", "stop and don't ever start again" forever message. The forever message is a really hard one, especially for a nicotine addict.

But we know two things. Firstly, that people who can successfully quit for four weeks are more likely to be able to give up permanently. This is because the hardest battle is with the cravings, which weaken after the first couple of weeks. Secondly, humans are wired to think more in the short-term. A short challenge with a fixed end date, such as a week, two weeks or a month, is easier to comprehend and more compelling to try than something that rolls on forever. It's not all-or-nothing any more. Instead, it's a "try it for a bit and see if you can stretch it out a bit longer".

In a similar way, companies like Amazon Prime and Netflix take this approach too. They aim to shape longer-term consumer behaviour by offering customers a short-term free trial in the hope that by the time the free trial ends the customer will have reshaped some of their viewing and buying behaviours and will want to continue their subscription.

If you are encouraging a long-term change in customer behaviour, can you start with a short-term challenge? Then work on stretching it once customers have experienced the benefits.

When we're excited about a big day or an important event, such as a birthday, a wedding, or a holiday, it can seem such a long way away that it feels as though the day will never arrive. In such circumstances we find ourselves creating countdowns, chunking down time so it feels more imminent than it is. For example, every year, millions of people count down their days through December to Christmas Day with an advent calendar.

If the experience you provide your customers is a long way away, can you create a more immediate state of anticipation, or chunk down the waiting time so it doesn't seem so long?

Chunking down time creates an illusion of speed

experience

Pronunciation: /ik'spɪərɪəns/

noun: an event or occurance that leaves an impression on someone

A customer's experience of a service is the lasting impression they have of it. It's based on the sum of all the interactions they have had with it.

It's shaped by the way all of their senses were engaged and how they felt about the service at each stage. Customer experiences are based on people's expectations of the service, which can be influenced by the experiences and stories of others.

Every service has an "experience", whether it has been thoughtfully considered (engineered, even) or not.

What is your customer experience? Start by thinking about your values and what your purpose in the world is. Then think of all the ways you can immerse someone in that world in a positive and immediate way. A great way to think about your customer experience is to complete this line…

The _____ experience

↖ insert name of your service here

…and then consider in detail how amazing that experience can be.

Learning to pour a perfect
glass of Heineken beer

Heineken Experience, Amsterdam

Flying an Airbus A380
Emirates Aviation Experience, London

Recreating the home sound
experience

SONOS, New York City

The Heineken Experience in Amsterdam started as the Heineken Museum in its working factory on the outskirts of the city centre. When it outgrew the factory and relocated out of the city, it took the chance to revitalise the old space and turned it into the Heineken Experience. Rather than static displays, Heineken brings its brand to life in an immersive, vibrant, hands-on way, connecting visitors to its key values around quality, excellence, family and most of all, fun.

It hires confident storytellers as guides, often young people who work in theatre. You don't have to be a beer drinker to get a lot from this experience. Note - you may go in as a person who doesn't like beer and come out as someone who does! (Like the author.)

Its multi-media "Brew You" ride takes customers through the brewing and bottling process where they become the beer! Later, they get an opportunity to buy a special edition bottle of the beer with their name on it.

Emirates is the key sponsor for the Emirates Air Line, the cable car that spans the River Thames, built for the 2012 London Olympic and Paralympic Games. At the North Greenwich terminal, you will find the Emirates Aviation Experience, a space filled with interactive games and immersive features that bring the experience of global travel to life. The experience has two aircraft simulators, a Boeing 747 and an Airbus 380. Your entry ticket is a genuine airline boarding pass and your flight simulator booking shows up on a departure board.

High-end audio retailer SONOS boasts an impressive experience store in SoHo, New York City, which resembles a listening boutique. The store contains a row of soundproof pods, each of which can be configured to represent various rooms in your home. Customers are invited to sit inside and use a touch-screen device to control the settings and immerse themselves in quality sound.

At all Disney theme parks, every ride starts with a queue. Depending on how busy the park is and the popularity of the ride, those queues can extend to well over an hour, which would be a terrible experience for visitors had Disney not found ways to entertain and delight them while they wait. Disney has mastered the queuing experience so well, building the story and raising the anticipation, that the wait is now an essential part of the ride itself, even on a quiet day.

After the ride, visitors take another route back to the main park via the gift shop. Part of this is logistical, to keep the flow of visitors moving. Another significant part is, of course, commercial, to encourage sales in the gift shop. But part of it is to satisfy a feeling of personal transformation following the ride. Leaving through a different exit adds to the sense of the journey. You are a different person when you leave.

If an experience is to be truly transformational, should customers leave through a different door to the one they came in?

Pay attention to the next experience you have in a bricks-and-mortar (physical) setting. What is the shape of the experience? Is it 'linear', where all customers follow the same path? Experiences like the Shrek Experience, the Heineken Experience, the London Dungeon, Windsor Castle, and IKEA stores are linear. Is it a 'gallery', like a store, or a museum where customers can move around freely in any direction, interacting with items in any order they choose?

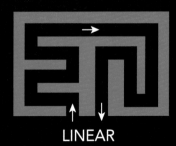

LINEAR

GALLERY

If you make your space linear, you control the story, its order and its pace.

Observe customers as they leave. You want to ensure they leave on a high (see Positive section, page 149). How animated are they as they leave? How are they walking? How fast are they talking? Can you read their expression? Pay extra attention to any differences in body language between people in the same group.

200 years ago, life expectancy was only about 40 years in the UK. Now, it's over 80, and it keeps going up[10]. With improving life expectancy, we actually gain approximately two extra hours of life per day, just from being alive.

It's like cashback

It's the best and worst cashback all at once. It's the best, because it's life. But it's the worst, because you have to wait your whole life to get it!

No one wants to wait their whole life for a benefit to show up

Some companies sell products that we do indeed wait our whole lives for. Life insurance policies and funeral plan products are the most obvious examples, but pensions and other financial products are far-long-term too. How do these companies make their products appealing to customers?

The answer is they market their products on the impact they have on key moments in the lives of their customers.

They talk about your graduation, buying your first home, bringing home your first baby, raising your family, staying close to the people who mean the most to you.

It's very emotional in content. They tell you they care about you, will support you and be there for you every step of the way.

They sell rational long-term products by talking about your life through the lens of emotional experiences. Look at their billboard advertising and watch their television commercials. Walk into any high street bank and look at the posters, banners and brochures on display.

Even the people who sell investments don't sell investments!

Puzzled by our inability to save for old age, our tendency to procrastinate and our apathetic attitude towards our future selves, a team at Stanford University set about using functioning magnetic resonance imaging (fMRI) technology to investigate what happens in our brains when we contemplate the future[11].

fMRI is a powerful tool that is used to measure brain activity by monitoring the tiny movements of blood that happen when a region of the brain is activated.

Different regions of the brain manage different types of activity and brain function. While there is still so much more to discover, decades of studies and meticulous mapping have enabled scientists to get a good understanding of what kind of neural activity each of these regions are responsible for.

The team at Stanford came across an exciting discovery in this study. It found that when people think about their future selves, the part of the brain that is activated is the exact same part that would be activated if you thought about someone you recognised but didn't know – such as a famous singer or movie star.

Quite literally, when we cast our imaginations into a future that doesn't exist yet, we see ourselves in the same way we see someone else. This appears to be one of the reasons we care more about our present selves than we do about our future selves. It explains the effect of the hyperbolic discount and our tendency towards here-and-now experience behaviour and away from investment behaviour. Our brains literally think someone else (our future selves) will pick up the tab for today's indulgences.

Your future self is still you!

The problem with the future is that it hasn't happened yet, so we can never fully anticipate how it will work out, but we can simulate scenarios to see how they fit our expectations. In a way, it's like bringing the future forward.

Fortunately, advancements in design, 3D technology, virtual reality simulation and computation are starting to give us these glimpses of our future lives.

☐ Architects and planners create photoreallistic images of what new buildings and community spaces will look like when completed.

☐ 3D technology has improved to a point where we can immerse ourselves in an alternative reality.

☐ IKEA and B&Q have an online virtual planning tool for kitchen and bathrooms respectively.

☐ Mydecco.com customers can plan a home improvement project and visualise the final result in a 3D simulation. They can even place items in their virtual room that can be bought for real.

☐ Using simulators, pilots can train to fly new aircraft even before the aircraft themselves have passed airworthiness tests.

☐ FaceApp, an app that spookily estimates what you will look like in the future, became one of the world's most popular apps in 2017.

☐ Clothing retailers are starting to adopt technology that will allow you to virtually try on their products.

☐ Online software can let you see what you would look like with a new hairstyle or a new pair of glasses.

Help customers to experience the future

It's considered unlucky to re-name a boat. In fact, it's not just unlucky, it's apparently an offence. According to sea-faring legend, when a boat is named, its details are added to a ledger maintained by Neptune (or Poseidon), the god of the sea. Changing a boat's name and having it floating around under its new assumed identity is therefore an act of fraud against the gods, and it appears Neptune is too busy with god duties to update his records.

Whether or not it is the result of offending the gods, any potential for bad luck at sea still sounds pretty bleak, which is why the ritual of naming a boat and the superstition of retaining its name is still so strong. There are sailors who will turn down the chance of owning a boat they love because they can't stand the name the previous owners gave it, and they refuse to change it.

Imagine if everything we did in life was like naming a boat, with no opportunity to change our minds afterwards. Imagine if you got just one opportunity to choose which subjects to study at school or university, which career to pursue, which sport to play, which person to date, which city and which house to live in, even which utility supplier or mobile phone company to buy from. It'd be pretty awful, right?

Decisions like these all require us to fast forward in time and ask our future selves if the choice we are making is still right for us. The problem is, we humans aren't very good at looking into the future and knowing what our future selves will want. We can only make hopeful projections based on what our today-selves want and value.

Will your future self still want today's choices?

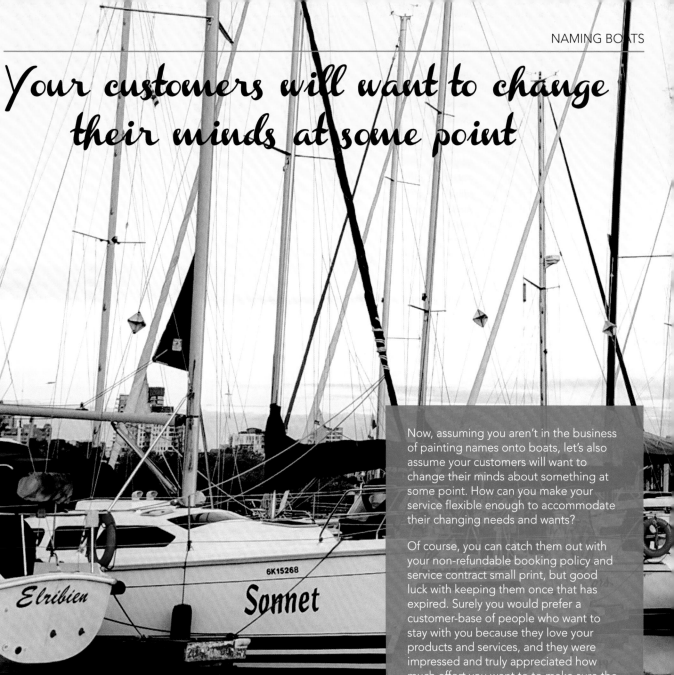

Your customers will want to change their minds at some point

Now, assuming you aren't in the business of painting names onto boats, let's also assume your customers will want to change their minds about something at some point. How can you make your service flexible enough to accommodate their changing needs and wants?

Of course, you can catch them out with your non-refundable booking policy and service contract small print, but good luck with keeping them once that has expired. Surely you would prefer a customer-base of people who want to stay with you because they love your products and services, and they were impressed and truly appreciated how much effort you went to to make sure the service they were experiencing was still the best fit for them.

Take customers on a quest

Breaking down a long-term goal into manageable tasks and challenges helps people to stay engaged

If customers are embarking on a long-term process, it can be made to feel more short-term by introducing levels to break it down into smaller steps.

If you learnt to swim through a formal programme, you will probably have started with your 5m badge. Then moved onto your 10m, 25m, 50m, 100m badges, and so on. You may have completed an extra award for life-saving skills such as treading water in your pyjamas for two minutes and diving to the bottom of the pool to retrieve a rubber brick.

BRONZE Weeks 1-5 **SILVER** Weeks 6-10 **GOLD** Weeks 11-15

Breaking down a long-term goal into manageable tasks and challenges helps customers to stay engaged. By chunking a large, difficult task into smaller pieces, it keeps the near future in their focus. It's a way of gaming the long-term into something that feels more immediate.

LEVEL UP!

Computer games apply this approach really well and are designed to hold players' interest and keep their motivation high. They introduce levels and increase degrees of difficulty as players progress. In alternative-world-type games, players are set quests, challenges, and mini tasks to perform to earn unique rewards. Simply wandering around a virtual world with nothing specific to do could become boring.

Examples of levels in action:

☐ Students studying for their degree focusing on the next assignment, the next semester…

☐ We have an education system broken down into "key stages".

☐ People who are trying to lose a lot of weight focus on the next half stone, the next stone, or the next 5% body weight.

☐ Long-term construction projects, such as the building of new highways and railroads, are described in phases.

☐ Long-term business plans are chunked down into quarterly targets. We use the language of milestones, conduct quarterly reviews and deliver long-term strategies in steps.

☐ Speaking of milestones… when travelling we break long journeys up by focusing on the next big town we'll pass. (It's literally what milestones are.)

☐ People wanting to learn a new language, or how to draw, or practise yoga are taught in classes ranging through beginner, intermediate and expert levels.

☐ Airlines have different levels of loyalty membership for passengers, based on the number of air miles they have and the frequency with which they travel.

Boost your miles...

People love boosts! Give customers a feeling of rapid progress by offering them a boost.

Can you enable them to check off some easy wins first? Give them a head start while they are highly motivated. Offer them a chance to gain extra loyalty points or air miles. Offer an intensive course to help them get started quickly on a new skill, such as learning to drive. Add an extra stamp or sticker to their coffee card so they are immediately nearer to their next free coffee.

"There'll be a sprint for the princesses!"

It's a little after 8am on a bus between the Disney World Florida resort hotels and the Magic Kingdom. The park doesn't open until 9am but there's an entertaining little ceremony as the park opens every morning, where Mickey and friends turn up on a steam train to open the main gates and welcome in visitors.

The ceremony is popular and the bus is already full. On board there is a mixture of excitement and anxiety, the kind you experience whenever it's first-come-first-served and you know it's going to be busy when you get there.

The bus is full of families of all kinds. Some with young kids, some with older kids, some with no kids, large families, small families, couples. Two women are sitting next to each other, talking. Each has a young girl dressed in her favourite Disney princess outfit.

"There's going to be a sprint for the princesses!" declares one of them.

Walt Disney World Florida has an app that draws live data from the park systems to tell customers how long the wait times are for each ride or experience, and there is one experience that always has a 100+ minute wait. All day. Every day.

Meeting the princesses.

No-one likes hanging around in a long queue. It's not only wasteful of customers' time, but in a place like Disney, where there is so much to do, it reduces the chance they have of enjoying all the experiences they want to during their visit. Being the first in line to meet the princesses is a pretty good tactic to reducing your wait time on the longest line.

But the location of the princesses isn't near the park entrance, and is instead several hundred metres into the park. As the gates open for the day, keen moms grab the hands of their little princesses and sprint up the street as predicted.

Or... take the vector

What if a wait is inevitable? What if customers can't have it straight away? Maybe your product or service is so bespoke, so unique, so specialist, it takes time. If what you deliver feels rushed, perhaps the customer will value it less.

Those idle moments while we waited used to be precious creative time, when our brains had to make up their own entertainment and we used to pay more attention to other people and our surroundings.

Instead of making customers feel compelled to always be switched on, always doing, always checking, responding and being notified, maybe we can help them to pause and to be present in the moment.

Rather than trying to align your service to our ever increasing pace of life, do the opposite.

Do the opposite

In what way can you slow customers down and enable them to be more present and connected and enjoy the experience?

Experience memory is like sensory memory

Imagine you are aiming to kick a football into an open goal. You have five balls, and you can kick each one in quick succession. If you miss the goal with the first ball you can correct your action for the second one and take a better strike to the target, and so on.

In the same way that we can temporarily store a memory like an image or a sound, we also have a temporary physical memory. It's often referred to as a muscle memory, and it can be refined over time with rehearsal to become a precise and repeatable action. It's actually neural activity in the brain rather than something stored in the muscles. Regardless of where the coding happens, the effect is the same - we get a short memory of the physical action we just performed, and an opportunity to adjust and improve in the moment.

In the TV game show "The Cube", contestants are challenged to complete a number of difficult physical tasks, often requiring precision and a steady hand. Examples of tasks include stacking narrow blocks on each other into a tower, moving around a space wearing a blindfold without knocking items over, and rolling a ball

along a tabletop in such a way that it passes a far point but doesn't fall over the edge. Contestants are told on average how many attempts it took other people to complete the task, and it's rare that a contestant will complete each one at the first attempt. They get ten lives.

If a contestant fails the challenge and they have remaining lives, they can have another go, in which case you would expect them to adjust their last action, perhaps push the ball a little softer or step a little further to the right...

They would if they could remember

In reality, the host Phillip Schofield engages them in conversation, asking them about their last attempt, how confident they are feeling and what a win would mean to them. By the time they get to try again, their muscles have forgotten the precision of their last action. It's as if they are trying for the first time every time.

storyline unrealistic and the ending too predictable.

Their opinion can't help but adjust your own memory of what you just saw. You think, "Maybe it wasn't all that great – I suppose they do have a point about the storyline."

Your friend may find your enthusiasm alters their memory too – "Perhaps it wasn't so bad – it's just a fun story after all." In that short window after an experience has ended, the opinion of another can shape how we remember it.

CINEMA

You have to lock in a good memory before it can be compromised

Waiting staff in restaurants checking if your meal is good aren't just looking for praise (and maybe a tip). They are taking an opportunity to correct course if there's a problem. When you are asked to give a star rating on the helpfulness of a web chat conversation or report the ease of an online transaction, the company is finding out what went well and what went wrong while you are still in the moment. Asking you after time has passed would mean it's not the full experience you will be evaluating, but your memory of it.

If the best moment to make an adjustment is while the action is still warm and the memory is still fresh, then your best opportunity to adjust course in the event your product or service fails to make its mark with your customers is as soon as possible.

How can you find out how well your product or service is performing (and correct course if necessary) while your customers are still in the moment?

☐ Do you promote your product or service as an investment or an experience? If it's the former, can you describe it in a more here-and-now, experiential way?

☐ Even if the main benefits are a long way off, can you at least make the headline about the short-term? It's okay to talk about the longer-term benefits – just don't make them the headlines.

☐ Draw a timeline of what customers will get if they access your service. What are the benefits in an hour? In a day? A week? A month? Three months? A year? Which of the more immediate benefits can you amplify?

☐ What is your today product? Most immediate benefits are emotional rather than physical - reassurance, connecting with others, a few smiles, a confidence boost, a listening ear, a first step and a plan, personal pride and satisfaction, a better night's sleep from now on, removal of pain, learning a new thing or skill...

☐ If you create a visual campaign... can you add some humour into the message? Advertisers often use humour as an instant reward for those who take the time to engage.

☐ If the main benefits are months away... you still have the power to provide an instant benefit... praise. What short-term authentic feedback can you give to customers to keep them motivated?

☐ Even banks selling investments don't talk about the long-term future. They talk about key moments in their customers' lives. What key moments in your customers' lives can you make better?

☐ Communicating a plan that is more than a few months into the future needs more than just enthusiasm. Can you find a way to help people to better visualise the future?

■ If the biggest benefits of your service to your customers are a long way into the future, can you somehow help them "experience the future" now?

■ We care less about our future selves than we do about ourselves today. It's as if we don't know they are the same person. Is there any way you can connect customers in a more compelling way to their future selves?

■ Do customers have idle time? On the phone? In a waiting room? In a queue? Can you make waiting more of an experience, or do you have a micro-task they can do?

■ Can you help customers get started more quickly? Perhaps you can remove any early steps they have to do, for example by simplifying registration or enabling online transactions, so that they can get started or make their purchase while they are still in the moment that inspired them.

■ Getting started can be the easy bit because it's when motivation is the highest. What additional support can you offer customers to keep them engaged after the initial buzz of getting started has faded?

■ Can you break down a long-term plan into smaller chunks, using levels and rewards, in a similar way to using swimming badges or levels on computer games?

■ If a customer has a very long-term goal, what short-term goal will help them get over the early hurdles? For example, stopping smoking for a month may feel like a more realistic challenge than stopping for a lifetime.

■ People appreciate "boosts". It helps them feel they are getting to their goal faster. They can boost air miles, loyalty points, progress... What boosts can you offer that your customer will love?

- "The _____ Experience". Imagine there is a physical space that you can use to represent your service or brand (maybe there already is), for example in an expo or a flagship store. Now can you describe in detail how awesome it is and how you use the space to help customers connect with your brand?

- If you have the physical space mentioned above, what shape is it? How do customers navigate their way around? Creating a linear experience puts you in control of the story, its order and its pace.

- Do you enable customers to change their minds? Can you make your service flexible enough to continue to meet their needs and wants over time?

- Can you help customers lock in a great memory of their experience with your service? Do it before it can be altered by someone else who had a different experience.

- Can you find out about a customer's experience while it's still fresh and you have a chance to put right anything that fell below their expectations? (Also, if the experience was great, you may get an extra testimonial to share!)

- Or… can you slow customers down? This section is all about how to draw the future closer, make use of micro-moments, speed things up. What if you were to find a way to slow customers down, to help them be more present, to pause and enjoy for once instead?

Certain

People prefer things they can
definitely have over things
they may or may not get

Red Wines

	125ml
Beaujolais Villages Chervet France 2016	8.40
Rioja Reserva Sonsierra Spain 2013	9.30
Malbec Perdriel Mendosa Argentina 2018	10.10
Valpolicella Super Ripasso Giaretta 2017	12.20
Pinot Noir Faively Burgundy France 2018	13.90

White Wines

	125ml
Vinho Verde Alvarinho Portugal IGT 2019	8.40
Pinot Bianco Venturin Veneto 2019	9.30
Gavi di Gavi Cortese Sparina DOCG 2019	10.10
Sauvignon Blanc Winkl Terlano Trentino 2019	12.20
Fiano Planeta Cometa DOC Sicily 2017	14.90

Have you ever considered how you select food from a menu when you are dining out? Do you thrive on the excitement of trying a new dish? Or do you prefer to go with what you know? Do you choose a dish you've had and enjoyed before? At least you know what you're getting. Perhaps you take a recommendation from other people in your party. Maybe you copy them, because what they just ordered sounds lovely. Maybe you want to know what dish the waiter walked past with on his way to another table - it looked amazing!

What about the wine to go with your meal? If you aren't an expert, choosing wine can be daunting. How do you choose wine? Do you go with a grape and a vintage you know you like? Do warm fuzzy memories of a recent holiday to a wine-making country influence your choice? Price is usually a good indicator. The more expensive the better - and no one wants to buy the cheapest one, right? Do you ask the waiter for suggestions? Ask what is popular? Or do you choose your wine the same way most people choose which horse to bet on - because you like the sound of its name?

What if you were buying wine from a supermarket where there are literally hundreds to choose from?

What if you aren't choosing for yourself? Instead it's a gift for a friend, or you want to take a bottle to a dinner party. How do you choose then?

Pay attention to the clues you look for next time you are choosing food or wine from a restaurant menu or a supermarket shelf.

> "Pick one with a security tag. If someone thinks it's stealable, it's probably drinkable."

Holidays are expensive outlays and we don't get to go on many of them, so we go to great lengths to make sure the ones we choose will give us the kind of experiences we are hoping for. We want them to be memorable for all the right reasons.

In the past, we used to visit a travel agent who would work with us to tailor a trip based on our preferences.

However, thanks to the internet, the power of information has shifted, and we can now assemble our own trips online. We can choose our own flights, hotels, ground transportation, meal packages and days out. But with all the given variables, this means there are literally millions of possible combinations we could assemble into a holiday, and if we want to have the perfect trip, it raises the pressure on us to choose well. That's when simplifications, shortcuts and decision tools come in handy for us.

Let's imagine you wish to book a holiday. How do you choose where you want to go, which airline you travel with and what you want to do when you get there?

Which factors influence you when choosing the trip you want to take? Which sources of information do you use?

- ☐ Price
- ☐ Star rating of hotel
- ☐ Direct flight from an airport near you
- ☐ Word of mouth from a friend
- ☐ Experience of a previous visit
- ☐ From a trusted source - such as a well-known holiday website or travel company
- ☐ Your past experience with an airline
- ☐ The predicted weather
- ☐ Photographs of the resort, rooms, pool, or nearby town
- ☐ TripAdvisor (or similar) reviews about the place you are thinking of staying

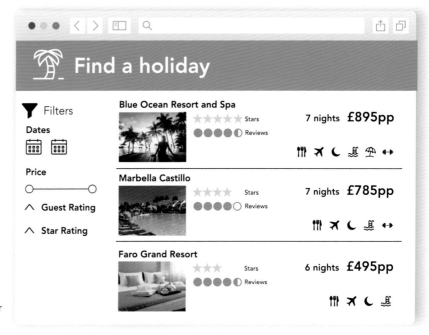

You might not think of it in this way, but all the steps we take when planning for a big purchase, like a holiday, are examples of us seeking certainty – so we know what we are going to get.

A couple of questions… Would you consider staying in a resort where you hadn't seen any pictures? Do you read reviews? (Do you continue to read reviews of the place you are staying after you have booked your trip? Or at that point do you not want to know if there is anything negative?)

Let's step up the ante a little. Having a bad experience on holiday is an expensive way not to have fun, but we can probably book another one next year. But what about those decisions that are rarer, and where the stakes are far higher? How do you choose your next job? Or your next home? How do you choose where your child attends school? How do they choose their university and the degree they want to do? How do you choose where you want to have your hip replacement operation carried out?

..and then there was Teletext

```
205        Teletext        Oct22 16:45:04
Majorca/Menorca/Ibiza              10/13
```

SPAIN HOLIDAYS

SEE P212

For inspiration and more great deals
visit teletextholidays.co.uk

Before we had the internet, smartphones and social media to waste our time on, we had Teletext. Teletext was a text-based information service that was broadcast alongside analogue television signals. It was popular in the 1980s and 1990s.

One of the great things about Teletext was the super-cheap holiday deals. Pages and pages of holidays. And, if you ever used Teletext, you'll remember each page could have lots of sub-pages within it. They rotated slowly, dwelling 20 seconds or so on each sub-page, just long enough for you to do a quick scan. If you saw something that demanded a longer look, you had to press "HOLD" on your TV's remote control to pause it, but you had to be quick, because if you missed it, you'd have to wait an age for it to come around again!

Allocate on arrival holidays

These were the extra-super-cheap travel deals you could find on Teletext, but you didn't know in advance where you were going to stay. You only knew which airport you were flying to and what the star-rating of the accommodation would be. They literally would allocate your accommodation on arrival based on what wasn't already sold out (there's the clue).

You'd rock up at the destination airport in the middle of the night, look for the travel rep who had your name on their list and then you'd all pile on a bus. Each time it stopped in the middle of nowhere, you'd wonder if it was your party getting off next. Your first task the next morning was to find out where on earth you were and what was nearby. Back then we didn't have Google Maps and inclusive overseas data roaming!

Of course, you could have bought a "named accommodation" package, where you knew which resort, hotel or apartments you would be staying at, but they were more expensive. Simply put, you can buy certainty.

```
377/06 ORACLE 377 Thu31 Dec ITV 2235:59
                                    6/12
```

GETAWAY 93

RESORT	DATE	NTS	ACCOM	ADLT	CHLD
IBIZA	26 MAY	07	S/C	£ 99	£ 49
MAJORCA	04 MAY	07	H/B	£105	£ 49
IBIZA	19 MAY	07	S/C	£ 99	£ 49
KOS	17 APR	07	R/O	£149	£129
IBIZA	05 MAY	07	S/C	£ 89	£ 49
RHODES	24 APR	07	R/O	£149	£129
ZANTE	14 MAY	07	R/O	£149	£129

OPEN NEW YEARS DAY 11AM - 4PM

ACCESS   SWITCH

0302 761300

VISA   CONNECT

Ever since humans developed the ability to remember the past, and imagine a future that hasn't happened yet, we have become obsessed with trying to figure out what we're going to get and what the consequences of our actions and decisions will be. We are certainty-seekers.

If you're still to be convinced about the human desire for certainty, ask yourself if you've done any of the following:

- Enabled road traffic alerts on your car radio.

- Carried out a little ritual based on a superstition, like touching wood or throwing salt over your shoulder.

- Paid too much attention to polls.

- Listened to pundits speculate on the outcomes of sports fixtures.

- Written a letter to Santa, and then behaved through all of December – just in case.

- Read published reviews of products before buying, for example on Amazon, What Car or in Which Magazine.

- Asked friends for a recommendation, such as for a restaurant, a washing machine repair company, or a good nursery school.

- Raced to board a train so you were sure to get a seat and have somewhere to put your bags (or reserved seats in advance).

- Run to the boarding gate for an Easyjet or Ryanair flight so you got to sit next to the person you were travelling with, without having to fork out for priority boarding.

- Used a satnav or Google Maps to help you get to where you need to be in time. And set off extra early if it was an important trip.

Seems we all just want to know what we're going to get

It's easier than ever to be sure where you are and where you are going. No longer do you look at that little blue dot and have to walk up and down the street to figure out which direction you are facing.

Caxton St

Westminster A

Alarm +

07:00
Wake up

07:10
Get up

07:15
Definitely get up

junk sleep!

How many alarms do you set to wake you up each morning?

Multiple alarms offer more certainty that you'll wake up on time, but at the cost of several minutes of junk sleep every day. That's a pretty high cost.

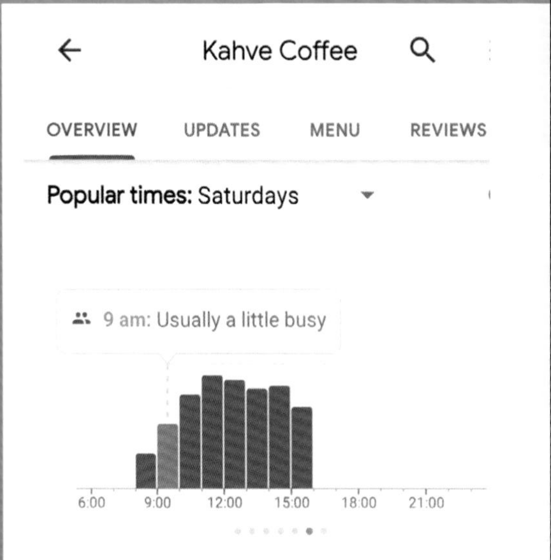

← Kahve Coffee 🔍

OVERVIEW   UPDATES   MENU   REVIEWS

Popular times: Saturdays ▾

👥 9 am: Usually a little busy

6:00   9:00   12:00   15:00   18:00   21:00

Google Maps will show you how busy your favourite restaurant, bar, cafe or shop is right now. So you know what to expect when you get there.

1 Harrow & Wealdstone   2 mins
2 Queen's Park   6 mins
3 Harrow & Wealdstone
                    14 32 10

Digital signs on the Underground in London tell you how many minutes you have to wait for the next train.

↑ Piccadilly line   Way out →

The subconscious mind is super-fast but error-prone. One of the many heuristics we apply on a daily basis is caused by a 'lazy' memory bias known as the "availability bias"[12].

The availability bias is based on the ease and speed at which an example or evidence of something springs to mind.

When the question comes up "how likely is it that [X] will happen?" there are two ways we can arrive at an answer. We can carry out our own research, delve into statistics and apply the logic, or we can apply a quick and dirty heuristic that says, "If it happens a lot, I must be able to remember examples of it. Can I remember an example of it happening?"

If we have to think hard to come up with more than one or two examples from memory, then we will concur from the mental effort required that it can't be that significant, it doesn't happen often, and it's not likely to happen now either. Note, we don't do this rationally, in fact, we are barely aware we did anything at all.

This is the reason why more people cancel their earthquake insurance the longer it has been since the last earthquake, which is statistically when the next one is more likely to happen, of course.

Countries all around the world were caught unprepared by the Covid-19 pandemic in 2020, despite frequent planning and monitoring by health organisations. Very few people alive today had experienced a pandemic before, and likely none of them had any real memory of the last one in 1919.

In April 1906 much of San Francisco was destroyed and thousands of lives lost in a huge earthquake. The West Coast of North America is braced for another "big event", predicted to happen any time in the next 15-20 years. Yet, it will feel less likely to happen, because no one can recall anything like the 1906 earthquake.

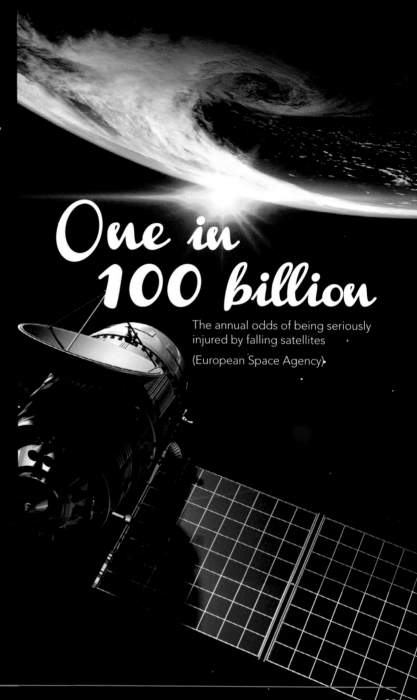

In October 2011, the newsrooms were full of reports that an old NASA satellite was due to fall back into Earth's atmosphere and that a small piece, the size of a washing machine or a small van, would likely make it through re-entry and come crashing back down onto Earth's surface somewhere. News studios entertained experts and discussed how big a splash or how big a dent the piece of space junk would make, depending on where it landed, and discussed the risk it posed to life on Earth.

They talked about how fast it would be travelling, what noise it would make and whether we would see it in time to get out of its way if we happened to be the unfortunate individual under its path.

One in 100 billion.

According to the European Space Agency, that's the approximate annual odds of being severely injured by falling satellites. (It's probably similar to the annual odds of being killed by falling satellites.) Incredibly small. So small, in fact, that we shouldn't have any column inches or airtime dedicated to a discussion about how we could save ourselves if we happened to be in its path.

It's another example of the availability bias. We believed it was more likely to happen to us because it was more prominent in our minds. This is due to the novelty of the example and that it's about space and NASA.

Satellites falling "out of control" to "smash" into Earth is also vividly and emotionally distinctive. Spending time listening to experts even talking about the possibility of being struck by one would make it feel more likely.

Note: We didn't get to find out where the satellite landed. Both it, and all the media stories surrounding it, vanished a day or so later.

One in 100 billion

The annual odds of being seriously injured by falling satellites

(European Space Agency)

One in 45,057,474 - that's the odds of winning the jackpot in Lotto, the UK's national lottery draw. It's the odds of correctly guessing all six balls, drawn out of 59 possible numbers.

1 chance in 45,057,474

It used to be one in about 14 million, which is bad enough, but in October 2015, the jackpot became three times harder to win with the addition of ten extra balls to choose from.

Lotto claimed the change would make it "more exciting" for players. (Its staff need to get out more.) They also said there would be bigger prizes and more frequent rollovers. Of course, on this it was right - because with an average 14 million players each week, and a one in 45 million chance of winning, there are a lot of rollover weeks.

The chances of winning are miniscule, deceptively low, too tiny to comprehend, but since the draw began in 1994, over 3,500 winners have become instant millionaires. Those 3,500 winners include many people, just like us, with backgrounds like ours, and stories like ours, who took a chance, bought a ticket, and won.

We believe something is more likely because we can vividly recall an example of when it happened. We see the winners' excited faces, holding an oversized cheque for the press photographs and wonder what we would do with all that money if one day we won too. It's no surprise that we believe that our chances of winning are so high.

If you still feel the need to play, there are three tips for you on the next page.

1 Don't use numbers 1-6

1, 2, 3, 4, 5, 6. It's true they are just as likely as any other combination of six numbers to be drawn, but, according to Lotto, about 10,000 people choose them each week just to make a point and if these numbers ever did come up, your share of the jackpot would be pretty tiny. That would be a real waste of good luck.

2 If you must buy a ticket, make it Euromillions on a Tuesday

Euromillions has a £1 million UK raffle with every draw. One ticket drawn at random wins £1 million. The odds of winning the raffle are, of course, based on the number of players - the fewer the players, the better your chances. So, you want to choose the draw with the least number of players, which is the Tuesday draw.

In fact, you want to buy your Tuesday ticket immediately after a huge jackpot has been won on a Friday because people buy fewer tickets when the jackpot is smaller. (Forget about the jackpot itself, the odds of that are one in 116,000,000.)

3 Don't use the same numbers every week

There are people who have used the same line of numbers every week for the last 20+ years, since it began. While they have probably long passed the point where they think they will actually win the jackpot, they are terrified of missing even a single draw, in the belief that the one time they don't buy their ticket will be the week their numbers finally come up. If you use the same numbers every week, those numbers will become etched in your memory, and you won't be able to escape the knowledge that you would have won.

Lotto used to only be drawn on a Saturday. When the Wednesday draw was added, people said they wouldn't do both... but they did, because what if their numbers came up on a Wednesday? Lotto increased the price per line from £1 to £2, and people said they would reduce the number of lines they played. But they didn't. Which set of numbers could players drop? Especially if they picked them for emotional reasons, such as their children's birthdays.

Which of your children is the luckiest?

Three top tips!
(if you still feel the need to play)

We live in a world of uncertainty and deal with the unknown every day. From big life decisions, such as what we want to study, our career choices, where and how we want to live and where we send our children to school, to smaller daily details, like the route we choose to drive to work, what we eat for dinner and which film to watch at the cinema. Each of these decisions is shaped by forces, such as convenience, pleasure and avoiding loss or harm, and most are taken at a subconscious level. They just "feel" right, and most of the time, this serves us perfectly well.

Often, though, we encounter situations where the risks are complex and our subconscious minds, which are not especially well-equipped for the logical detail, create shortcuts and make decisions based on biases and rules of thumb. We are not wired to automatically comprehend risk and chance. It requires both a rational, calculating mindset and the ability to think longer-term, something the previous emotional and short-term sections of this book has highlighted are not natural human strengths.

We deal with uncertainty every day

To sell insurance products, companies present us with a version of the future where things have gone wrong. They tell us about it in a story-like way, with real people talking about how awful it feels... (see emotional and positive principles).

At some point in that narrative, our subconscious minds reach a fear threshold, a fear that can be eliminated by purchasing another insurance product. We regularly buy without understanding the true odds (the base rate) of these things happening to us if we took no action at all.

When the stakes are high, making risk-based decisions under uncertainty is very difficult. Doubling your chance of developing a condition doesn't mean it's now definitely going to happen; reducing your chance of a rare illness by 50% could be a less effective survival strategy than reducing your risk of a more common health condition by even 2%.

As explained in previous pages, we are conditioned to want certainty, but we are terrible at understanding chance and probability.

In order for a risk-based message to have the desired impact, we first have to believe the consequence of the threat is severe, that there is a good chance the bad thing will happen to us, that changing our behaviour will lead to a different outcome and that we have the ability to change.

Unhelpful beliefs get in the way of the above. Our understanding of chance is shaped by our past experiences, our environment and how much we attribute our successes to our own ability rather than outside influences, such as luck or fate.

When we really struggle with changing a behaviour, like giving up smoking, for example, we can end up in a state of dissonance, where we know we are harming ourselves by our behaviour, but we can't find a way to change it. In such circumstances it's often easier for us to change our beliefs than our behaviour.

Changing the belief removes the tension we experience from the dissonance.

It's why you'll hear people saying things like this... (and believing it)

> Life expectancy is lower in this area. It's just how it is around here.

> I'm a great driver, I can text and drive quite easily.

> What goes around comes around.

> I wasn't breast-fed and I turned out okay.

> A 24-year-old died running a half marathon last week.

> "I'm lucky!"

> My great uncle smoked 60 a day and lived to 96.

> There's a lot of it in my family. It's inevitable I'll get it too.

> I'll definitely start in the new year.

> I'll probably have started smoking again by next week.

> I've tried before and couldn't do it then.

Unhelpful beliefs create even *less certainty*

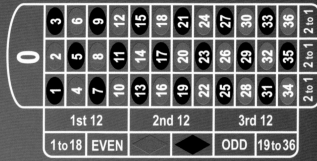

LAST 10: 8 32 0 4 33 1 20 26 7

What do you think will be next? Black or Red? Look at that long streak of reds. Of course, in roulette the odds of the next ball rolled landing on a red cannot be influenced at all by any of the previous outcomes. Roulette is total chance and each roll is a unique event in itself, yet most of us can't help but be influenced by what has happened before.

The longest streak on record in roulette happened at the Monte Carlo Casino in August 1939, when 26 consecutive blacks were returned. Gamblers lost millions of Francs betting on red because they believed a streak of blacks meant that a "re-balancing" must follow with extra reds. We appear to believe in a "law of small numbers"[13], meaning we expect a small sample to be representative of a larger sample. If we see a string of blacks on roulette, we will mistakenly believe more reds will follow to balance things out.

Higher or lower?

Is the next card in the sequence higher or lower than a six?

In the 1980s UK TV game show "Play Your Cards Right", contestants were challenged to correctly guess their way through a row of playing cards, deciding whether they thought the value of the next playing card would be higher or lower than the last. The players with the longest string of correct answers won. In a game like this, it is logical to always go for the answer with the greatest odds. For example, if you drew a five, the odds are greater the next card will be six or more, rather than four or less. It's basic probability. However, the odds of a whole series of cards always following the next most probable answer is unprobable in itself. Almost all contestants deviated from the most probable next answer at some point, based on nothing but 'gut feeling' (or the noisy insistence of the studio audience). In the end, winners were those with the luckiest guesses.

Infographics are illustrations and icons that help to convey information visually. If your key message is a data-heavy risk-related one, and customers need to make decisions based on them, you could find infographics to be a useful tool to help them understand their options and possible consequences.

Base rate and chance

These two circles show the reality of most risk reduction messages. Imagine the circle on the left is the ordinary risk of developing a long-term condition. Reducing the risk by 50% sounds worthwhile, but the base rate could be such that most people won't develop the condition anyway, and those who do change their behaviour may still develop it. Perversely, if customers have a better understanding of risk, it may actually disincentivise them from changing their behaviour at all.

Population odds

25% of the population (1 person in 4)

Composition

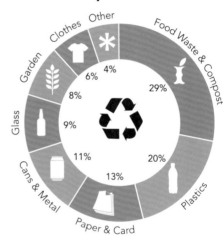

% Progress

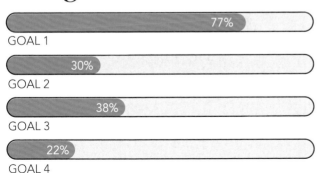

GOAL 1
GOAL 2
GOAL 3
GOAL 4

Percentage

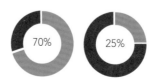

Comparison

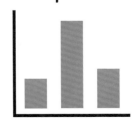

Two gentlemen waiting at a pedestrian crossing were talking about their favourite weather apps. One said that the app he used wasn't very accurate, but that he liked it because it always overestimated the chance of nice sunny weather and it made him feel happier.

Do you have a weather app on your smartphone? They are a great example of products we use to offer us some kind of certainty about the future.

Have you ever considered their use of probability for rainfall?

What does <5% risk of rain actually feel like?

The Met Office explained its 'probability of precipitation' as a useful opinion of the risk of rain:

> "If you are just hanging out your sheets that you need next week you might take the risk at 40% probability of precipitation, whereas if you are drying your best shirt that you need for an important dinner this evening then you might not hang it out at more than 10% probability."

Of course, don't we all make decisions this way?

If you live near the coast, you'll be used to seeing seagulls. You'll also know that at a certain time each year, their chicks are huge and they become particularly aggressive and poo on everything. Imagine now that the biggest risk to your freshly washed bed linen is no longer a bit of rain, but seagull poo! Imagine also that someone has devised an algorithm that can determine the percentage chance of seagull poo in any given hour where you live.

What is your threshold limit now?
15%, 5%, 1%...

Imagine you are presented with the following scenario. You can either have £1 million cash guaranteed OR you can enter a draw where you have a 10% chance of winning £10 million, an 80% chance of winning £1 million and a 10% chance of winning nothing at all.

Which option would you choose?

Option 1

£1 million cash guaranteed

Option 2

To enter a draw where there is a:

☐ 10% chance of winning £10 million

☐ 80% chance of winning £1 million

☐ 10% chance of winning nothing

In this hypothetical scenario, most people go for option one[14]. They choose the certainty of the £1 million. They probably reason that they are most likely to win £1 million anyway, and while £10 million is tempting, they decide not to chance it.

There's a chance of losing

If everyone was to choose Option 2, there would be more money in the system. For every 100 people, the prize fund would be £180 million for Option 2, instead of £100 million for Option 1, so that certainty we want comes at a cost.

But what if it was just £10?

What if the prize was based around a much more modest sum of £10, and the prize draw on offer in Option 2 was now £100, £10 and £0 respectively?

Given the new scenario, most people switch their choice to Option 2. Here, they reason that £10 is such a small amount they might as well gamble in the hope of the larger win.

Think about the difference between £1 million and £10 in terms of certainty...

Probability language refers to the choice of words we use when we're trying to convey to another person the likelihood of us doing something, or of something happening. We're highly sensitive to it and use it effortlessly.

Look at the group of words below. Put them in order from weak to strong, based on the likelihood they convey. For example, if you think someone saying "I'll probably attend" signals a greater likelihood than if they say "I'll possibly attend", then you'd list "probably" as stronger than "possibly".

certain intend to possibly promise maybe chance might try definitely will probably somewhat hope likely guaranteed consider

Few people will put all of these words in exactly the same order, but your top few probably included, "guaranteed", "definitely" and "certain", and your bottom ones included the words "hope", "consider", "intend to" and "try".

Let's imagine someone invites you to an event. You're not sure if you want to go and you don't want to upset the host. You may find yourself using words like "maybe" or "possibly" in your reply. We also effortlessly add nuance to these words. "I'm sure" is stronger than "I'm pretty sure".

A sign you aren't fully confident in the service or product you offer is when you water down your language and say things like "maybe", "try to" and "possibly". "Our role is to help", "to support", "sometimes this happens", "you might find"…

You want customers to know they are going to benefit hugely from your service or product, or even be transformed by it. (Or else what are you designing it for?)

Check to see if you are using weak probability language. If you find any, can you use stronger words instead?

Can you use stronger words?

"Let me help you with that"

When challenged to consider their customers' point of view, many organisations describe what their products and services do in terms of helping their customers. "We help our customers look great at an important event." "We help customers learn to drive." "We help customers to get fitter." "We help customers choose the right insurance cover."

Helping people is a good thing (of course), but the word "help" is a fluid term. "Let me help you with that…" can be used in the following contexts:

1 "Let me do that for you."
E.g. When someone from tech support sets up your email account on your smartphone for you.

2 "Let me show you how to do that."
E.g. When someone shows you how to use the self-service check-in machine at an airport.

3 "Let me point you in the right direction." E.g. When a stranger tells you the best way to get to the railway station.

Number three comes with unfortunate subtext - "I can point you in the right direction… but really you're on your own!"

When the responsibility for the final result lies with the customer - for example, if they are losing weight or saving money - then the word "help" can reflect a lack of confidence.

If you use the word "help" to describe your product or service, swap it for a stronger, more certain, alternative.

For example, instead of "We help customers choose the right insurance cover" say "We make sure our customers get the right insurance cover."

Guarantees are super-certainty and we naturally find them appealing. Seeing a guarantee on a product gives us an added sense of certainty that we are making a good purchase. Some companies go beyond their legal obligations, for example, John Lewis offers an extra year guarantee on electronics and electricals over and above what the manufacturers supply. Kia Motors offers motorists a seven year warranty, way above the industry standard of three years. Companies find our desire for greater certainty can be levered for a competitive advantage.

That's all very well for physical products, but when it comes to providing services that require some effort on the customer's part, such as studying for a degree or taking part in a fitness class, adding a guarantee requires a bit more thought.

A service may say... "We can't guarantee anything! We don't know what customers will do or how hard they will try... and even if they did everything we advise, we can't guarantee they will succeed...."

...because they are focusing on factors out of their control, including the final outcome.

Guarantees are Super-certainty

An athlete will never say they are going to win, even if they believe it's true. What you'll hear instead is a guarantee to "do my best" and "give my all". They understand that many things in competition are out of their control. They don't know how their competitors will perform, or if there will be other factors at play that will impact the final result, especially in sports where there is such a fine line between winning and crashing out! Instead, they focus on the things they can control, such as their style, their technique, their ability to stick to a race strategy and their effort to try their hardest.

A guarantee to try!

Taking a lesson from athletes, you can guarantee what you control, and you may find there's quite a lot you control...

- A call back to customers within 30 minutes.

- A pleasant, smiling person to greet customers at reception.

- Clean and tidy fitting rooms.

- Products delivered within a day.

- A confirmed place on the course they booked.

- A short wait time to get started from any referral.

- Impartial advice.

- That you will price-match your competitors for the same service.

- That your team have been trained to a high standard.

- That classes, appointments or journeys start or depart on time.

- That you will be open or available when you say you are (literally, your opening hours).

What can you guarantee? ...and are you brave enough?

EXPERIENCE GUARANTEES

UK hotel chain Premier Inn guarantees a great night's sleep. If you don't have a great night's sleep it will give you your money back. You may think people will stay there and deliberately complain about anything to get their money back. But, apparently that's not the case. Instead, it's a draw. Customers are mostly decent, and appreciate the effort a hotel will go to to be able to make that kind of promise.

Premier Inn is guaranteeing its customers' subjective experience of a good night's sleep, a thing it can't control, but clearly something it is very confident it can still deliver. And people find that level of confidence and certainty very appealing.

Costa Coffee (part of the same parent company as Premier Inn) offer its "Never a Dull Taste" guarantee. Simply, if you don't like the taste of your coffee, it promises to remake it how you like it. It's another guarantee of a subjective experience.

Guaranteeing experiences that you don't control shows you have very high confidence in the quality and effectiveness of what you offer.

What about the things you don't control?

What great experience guarantee can you make?

Before you think that this is a highway to a high court fight, think for a moment what a guarantee actually is. It's not an absolute certainty that things will work, it's a promise of what you will do in the event it doesn't. It's a two-part promise:

Part 1 – You make a promise you are very confident you can keep
Part 2 – You say what you will do to put it right if it goes wrong

Do products and services fail? Yes, of course

What could your experience guarantee look like?

- **Bubble bath -** We guarantee you will feel relaxed after a soak in our bubble bath, or bring the rest of the bottle back for your money back.

- **Yoga studio -** We guarantee that you will feel amazing after your yoga class, or we invite you to come and tell us where it fell short of your expectations and will give you your money back.

- **Driving school -** We are so confident in the quality of our instructors that we guarantee you will pass your driving test first time, or the next three lessons are on us.

- **Rail company -** We guarantee you will enjoy your train journey today, or we invite you to come and tell us how we can improve it and we'll give you a voucher towards future travel.

- **Visitor attraction -** We guarantee you will have a great experience with us, or we invite you to meet our director for a coffee and you can tell us where we fell short.

> If your product or service fails, take the opportunity to talk to customers about how you can put it right for them

Guaranteeing someone else's experience takes courage but your confidence will draw in more customers. If the experience falls short, you are presented with an excellent opportunity to have a conversation with customers about where you didn't meet their expectations.

What are you so confident you can deliver well? What experience can you guarantee?

Now are you brave enough?

Can you name Santa's reindeer?

(Answers on page 117)

When you think about it, it's a remarkable story, that every year on Christmas Eve, Santa Claus delivers gifts to all the children around thre world, travelling on a sleigh pulled by magic, flying reindeer.

What's remarkable about the story isn't the many ways in which it goes beyond the edges of science, even with supersonic reindeer, but in the consistency with which we tell it. It's remarkable that grown up people all around the world can not only easily recite the story, but we even know the names of his fictional reindeer. (There was a spoiler alert!)

That consistency is part of the proof we offer to children to persuade them he is real. If we each had a slightly different version of the story, then children would compare notes and we'd be rumbled.

Proof of Santa

What evidence do we offer children to prove that Santa exists?

☐ They see him in movies, TV commercials, posters, products, books and magazines. He looks exactly the same every time - red coat and hat, white trim, black belt and boots - thanks Coca-Cola!

☐ We sing songs about him.

☐ We take them to actually meet the guy!

☐ If they realise the Santa they just met is a person in a costume, we are ready with tales about how busy the real Santa is.

☐ They write to him and tell him which toy they wish for as a gift... and then it appears!

☐ But the main reason they believe he exists is simply because we say he does, and we all say it. All the grown ups tell the same story to all the children. We have an unwritten social code that says it's not okay for us to tell anyone else's child that Santa doesn't exist.

You'd have to be a very cynical child to figure this one out for yourself

SPOILER ALERT ⚠

In 1955, a young girl accidentally dialled the unlisted phone number for the Continental Air Defense Command (CONAD) operations centre in Colorado Springs in the USA, believing she was calling Santa Claus. The quick-thinking commander on duty realised what was happening and assured the young girl that they would make sure Santa safely completed his journey. Now known as NORAD, is has continued to enable children and families to track Santa on Christmas Eve ever since.

Obviously, times have changed a little over the last 65 years, and NORAD now provides the facility to track Santa online (noradsanta.org) and on Facebook, Twitter, YouTube and Instagram. If you're worried you'll get caught out by not having gifts under the tree when NORAD says he has already visited, then you might want to stop little ones taking tablet devices to bed on Christmas Eve.

In nature, some animals have features that make them attractive to potential mates, but which at first glance appear to be an evolutionary disadvantage. An example is the peacock, whose extra-large and vibrantly coloured tail feathers are used to signal to peahens their suitability as a mate.

The problem is the very same display of bright feathers also catches the eye of predators, and their long length makes it hard to sprint away!

Why, then, would peahens find this so attractive? It's because the disadvantage is so great the peacock must be a top specimen just to be alive[15]. And it's a signal that can't be faked.

In our commercial world, honest signals convey value to customers. We look for ways to prove to them that our products are genuine and well made. Counterfeiters of luxury goods work hard to mimick those delicately crafted signals.

Honest signals are not just in the details of physical products, but any way in which you can demonstrate honestly to customers you went above and beyond in providing your service to them. In what way can you undeniably demonstrate how much effort you have put into making sure they have a great experience?

Show customers how superior your products and services are in a way it would be impossible to fake

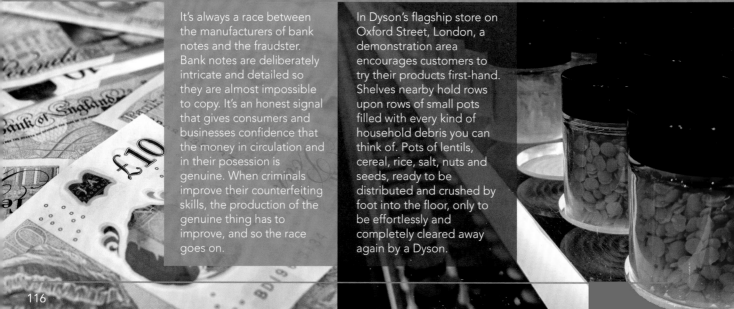

It's always a race between the manufacturers of bank notes and the fraudster. Bank notes are deliberately intricate and detailed so they are almost impossible to copy. It's an honest signal that gives consumers and businesses confidence that the money in circulation and in their posession is genuine. When criminals improve their counterfeiting skills, the production of the genuine thing has to improve, and so the race goes on.

In Dyson's flagship store on Oxford Street, London, a demonstration area encourages customers to try their products first-hand. Shelves nearby hold rows upon rows of small pots filled with every kind of household debris you can think of. Pots of lentils, cereal, rice, salt, nuts and seeds, ready to be distributed and crushed by foot into the floor, only to be effortlessly and completely cleared away again by a Dyson.

Customers need assurance that they are right to be buying from you, especially if the purchase they are making is expensive or particularly important. How can you take away the risk for them of making a bad choice so they can have confidence they are choosing the right thing?

Some examples:

- A free trial period for media streaming services, such as Netflix, Amazon Prime, Audible and Spotify.

- eCommerce sites that offer free postal delivery on goods, and free postal returns if you don't want to keep them.

- The first session free at a fitness studio.

- A test drive in a new car.

- Free samples or swatches of carpet or sofa fabrics to test and compare (and stroke).

- Free samples of things to eat, like cheese or a tiny piece of a new cake at a coffee shop.

- Stores that have a generous returns policy if you change your mind.

- Restaurants or hotels that let you cancel your reservation.

- Free adjustments on garments if they aren't the right fit first time. For example, Levis will adjust the length of your new jeans for free if they aren't quite the right length for you.

- Adding a guarantee to a product or service so customers know what to do if it doesn't live up to their expectation.

De-risk the choices your customers make

(From page 114, Santa's reindeer: Dasher, Dancer, Prancer, Vixen, Comet, Cupid, Donner, Blitzen and Rudolph.)

Buy 9 coffees get the 10th FREE!

1 2 3 4 5
6 7 8 9 FREE

If the final outcome isn't certain, then elements of certainty can be applied in a different way.

"if you do... we will..."

Some coffee shops offer loyalty cards where customers receive a free coffee if they complete a card, gaining a stamp for each coffee they buy. The certainty isn't in the quality or taste of the coffee itself, but in the promise the café makes to customers of the reward they can have for buying them.

You don't have to like coffee; you don't even have to drink it!

Can you offer rewards or points for attendance or adherence? A special level membership for attending 20 aqua aerobics classes, a t-shirt for completing a charity run, extra loyalty points (or boosts) for buying particular products? Loyalty schemes, points collection and rewards can provide a different kind of certainty for customers' actions.

Book it in...

Booking an appointment adds a level of certainty, even if it's just a commitment between friends.

'Drop-in' services offer certainty too - letting people know they will definitely be seen if they call in at certain times of the week.

JUNE

S	M	T	W	T	F	S
	1	2	3	4	5	6
7	8	9	10	11	12	13
14	15	16	17	18	**19**	20
21	22	23	24	25	26	27	28
29	30	24				

or check in!

Location-based social networking "games", such as Foursquare, allow people to share their progress with each other and earn badges and points for achievements.

Let's be clear... there are no tangible benefits to collecting virtual badges. A greyscale icon becomes a colour icon. But people will go to huge lengths to collect them.

new cooker being installed

Airlines operate a strict time schedule for arrivals and departures to minimise airport overheads and maximise time in the air. They don't make money while aircraft are on the ground. It requires speedy disembarking, offloading, cleaning, refuelling, reloading and boarding. Airlines need passengers to be ready and waiting to board their flight when called, not browsing through the duty-free or having an extra drink at the airport bar.

Aviation enthusiasts everywhere can now download flight tracking apps to their smartphones and tablets and monitor the movement of aircraft across the skies. What do you do when you know the inbound aircraft you will be departing on is still an hour away from arriving, and yet the airline has already called you to the gate?

Train operators at London's main terminus railway stations often have trains already on the platform for a while before the platform number is displayed to passengers. This time is used to clean the train from the inbound service and enable staff time to change shifts and prepare for the next journey ahead.

Passengers of busy services want to be first to board so they can get a seat and somewhere to put their luggage (classic certainty behaviour). If they find out the platform number too soon, they show up, causing problems for staff trying to do their work and it can be dangerous.

However, the API data source that informs the rail network is also consumed by Google and used in Google Maps. If you are a rail commuter in London and hoping to be first on board, you can get a head start by looking at your journey on Google Maps to find your departure platform long before it's shared with everybody else.

Customers' ability to get their hands on data about aspects of your business processes will only increase. They will invariably get hold of information that increases their convenience but makes your work harder. Rather than pretend they don't know it, how can you adjust your customer experience to accommodate it?

How can you make it part of the customer experience?

There is a downside to certainty.

And that is that if you only ever get exactly what you are expecting, there is no room left for surprise and delight. There's no chance of discovering something exciting and intriguing.

Think of an occasion when you received a surprise gift, but somehow you had already found out about it in advance, so you had to pretend it was a surprise. Worse, you didn't like the gift, but you still had to pretend it was the best surprise ever… how did you show surprise?

Eyebrows up, eyes wide, mouth opens, jaw drops, sharp intake of breath, head back. Add a little squeal of joy if you can muster it. The surprise response is a universal one. We all recognise it and we've all tried and failed at some point to fake it.

When we're surprised, it means we experienced something we didn't predict. The surprise response is designed to allow us to take in the maximum amount of information very fast. Eyes wide, head back, intake of breath… It allows us to work out in a split second if the unexpected thing is going to harm us or not. And then we commit the new thing to memory, where it can be stored to help us predict better in future.

Surprise and delight are excellent mechanisms for creating strong memories and for adding lasting impact to messages. They are the inspiration for stories shared between friends, making them a fantastic source of word-of-mouth marketing.

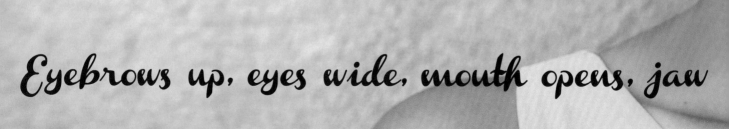

Eyebrows up, eyes wide, mouth opens, jaw

The same surprise response is experienced when a comedian tells a joke. Jokes are told in two parts. Firstly, the set up, which sets the context, and then the punchline. The punchline is where the humour lies and it only works if it's not what you were expecting.

The theory is that laughter is a relief response that follows a surprise. Basically, we have the surprise moment, and once we realise the new thing isn't going to harm us, we experience relief, and it shows up as laughter.

Have you ever laughed uncontrollably on a rollercoaster ride?

This chapter has encouraged you to look at the work you do and the customers you serve through the lens of certainty and to add more certainty and assurance where you can.

But don't forget to make space for surprise, delight and discovery

drops, sharp intake of breath, head back

- [ ] Do you use risk-based messages to try to draw customers to your product or service? Do you think this message really resonates with them or can you find a better way of framing it to add more certainty?

- [ ] What kind of clues do customers look for to feel confident they are doing the right thing choosing your product or service? This is especially true if what you offer is a high-stakes "purchase", like a holiday, a home or whether or not to have an operation. How can you help them be certain they made the right decision?

- [ ] How can you offer customers more certainty? Perhaps a reserved parking space, lots of pictures and descriptions on your website, or links to honest reviews from other customers.

- [ ] Can you offer more certainty still, even if that makes it a premium product? People will pay for extra certainty.

- [ ] What kind of certainty behaviour do your customers exhibit? For example, people run to board trains so they can get a seat and have somewhere to put their luggage. If you look at customer behaviour through the lens of certainty, you will find clues to where you can improve their experience.

- [ ] What kind of unhelpful beliefs get in the way of people accessing your service?

- [ ] How do you use probability language? This is language we use when we are trying to convey to others the chance of something happening. Do you use weak probability language? This could give the impression you lack confidence in what you deliver. Customers are drawn to stronger probability language and greater certainty.

- Can you use infographics or digital tools to help customers understand potential future risks and likely outcomes?

- Are you brave enough to offer a guarantee? People are reassured by guarantees on a service or product. It tells them the provider or manufacturer is confident their product is high quality. (Hint: You can guarantee what you control.)

- What about guaranteeing what you don't control? This demonstrates an extraordinary confidence that customers will love their experience.

- If the guarantee is not met, how can you put it right for customers? "If we fall short of your expectations, this is what we'll do…"

- Are you consistent? Consistency is a level of certainty that tells customers what to expect and how to engage with your product or service. Consistent brand, consistent language, consistent experience.

☐ People think something is more likely to happen if they can easily recall an example of it happening before. Can you create a vivid and emotional example of your service or product in use?

☐ Can you demonstrate to customers how superior your product or service is in a way that would be impossible to fake?

☐ Can you de-risk the choice your customers make when they buy from you? Free delivery, free returns, samples, test drives…

☐ Can you offer rewards, or points for attendance or adherence?

☐ Can you offer appointments for those customers who want them? Anchoring a time in the diary provides certainty for customers. If you don't offer appointments, telling customers when they can access your service is also a level of certainty.

☐ In your customers' drive for more certainty, they will sometimes have access to information you'd prefer they didn't have. How can you work with that and make it part of the experience?

☐ Making everything about your product or service certain is a double-edged proposition. Customers want to know what to expect, but you don't want to become dull. Are you leaving space to surprise and delight your customers? It's the thing they will talk about when they next have a catch up with their friends.

Positive

People prefer to work
towards the things they want
than away from the things
they don't want

"You need to do more of X, or Y will happen."

The 'lesser evil' type of message is everywhere. Buy insurance or… one day your house will burn, or you'll crash your car, or your pet will become ill and you'll be on your own to deal with it. Take greater care of your health or… one day you'll have diabetes, or have circulatory disease, or have a stroke. Feed your kids better, or you might outlive them. Take away their smartphones and make them play sports, or they will have no social skills when they grow up. Make them go to school, or you'll be fined or go to prison. Pay into a savings account and start a pension as soon as you can, or you'll be broke when you retire…

We've all heard these messages and regardless of their truth, they never make us feel good.

(the thing we're encouraging) → $X < Y$ ← (what happens if you don't)

The problem is in the construction of the message. It comes with hidden subtext, suggesting that the action we are encouraging, X, is unpleasant, just not quite as awful as Y.

Let's take walking as an example. We are told to walk more, aiming for 10,000 steps a day, to help us be less likely to get a string of long-term conditions. But actually, walking is quite a nice thing to do on its own. Why would we beat people up with a negative message about doing something they might enjoy anyway?

This is not to say that negative motivators don't work – they certainly do! People are hugely motivated to avoid a loss. But if you are only doing something to avoid a greater evil, then you will never intrinsically enjoy it for its own sake.

There's another problem with this… it's probably not just one single X. That implies X is a one-off thing. You don't just make one payment into your savings, you don't just attend one class, you don't just get one early night, you don't just sacrifice one evening of alcohol, or one cigarette, or one takeaway. You don't recycle one glass bottle, spend one evening revising, work one overtime shift…

It could be 100X or 1000X, or more. You might need to do X repeatedly over a really long period of time to avoid Y.

Maybe they just can't be compared

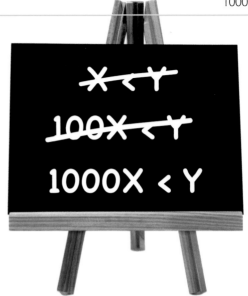

People simply do not enjoy doing something out of fear of something worse. But they do enjoy working towards the things they actually want. It feels nicer to work towards something we want rather than away from something we don't want, and often the difference is a simple reframing.

So, in what amazing ways will your service or product change your customers' lives?

Will it make their confidence skyrocket? Will it help them sleep? Maybe concentrate better? Feel better about themselves? Give them an uplift of energy? Make their day easier? Make their children happier? Make their friends admire them more? Help them master a cool new skill? Enable them to unlock the next step in their dream career?

Forget the negativity, you'd be better off making X more desirable.

Tell us the good stuff!

What if "Y" isn't so terrible?

There's another flaw in the X < Y negative style of promoting a service or product. The approach only works if we remain afraid of the possibility of the terrible thing happening to us and we don't find an easier alternative to solve it (such as taking a pill to reduce our blood pressure rather than getting fitter).

Over time, we may realise the really bad outcome, Y, is unlikely to happen to us, or that the impact of it is not as awful as we first thought, making us less afraid of it.

It feels nicer to say "yes" than to say "no".

In the 2014 referendum on Scottish independence, the psychological advantage of the "Yes campaign" was referred to frequently.

Who wouldn't want a bottle of that?

Physical activity is a great example of a product that in itself is intrinsically positive and upbeat. Yet in the drive to get people moving more often, it's usually promoted and talked about in the negative context of reducing disease and life-changing or life-limiting health conditions.

If people really want the benefits of a change in behaviour enough, they will make the effort for that change. But it must be something they really want.

If the benefits of physical activity could be bottled and sold, it would be a best seller!!

Ingredients:

☐ Sense of wellness

☐ Confidence

☐ Better condition of skin, hair and nails

☐ Energy boost

☐ Longer life

☐ Increased vitality

☐ Better sleep

☐ Feel-good endorphins

In 2016, the verb "adulting" made an entry into the Oxford English Dictionary after being shortlisted for word of the year.

Adulting is informally used to describe things responsible grown-ups have to deal with, such as fixing a leaking boiler, paying bills, getting up early to go to work, and completing tax returns. A quick search for the hashtag #adulting on any social media channel will bring up funny examples.

Our desire to continue to act like children, even when we are grown-up, shows that we are programmed to want to enjoy ourselves and to seek out fun. We find the opportunity for fun so appealing that a multi-billion-dollar global entertainment industry has been built to supply it.

Theme parks, adventure lands, amusement arcades, funfairs, cinema, home entertainment, gaming... The clues are all in the title. We'll even pay a lot of money if our anticipation of the fun we'll have is high enough.

In what way can you make your products and services and brand more fun?

Note: Beware of trying too hard to engineer fun. The best fun is experienced organically, you just need to create the environment in which it can happen.

131

A participant in bootcamp sessions described how three times per week she gets up at 5.30am and is at the beach by 6.15am. Then she slogs her way through an incredibly tough 45 minute workout. What makes her do it?

She said, "I can't tell you how amazing I feel at 7am!"

She was addicted to the buzz feeling she got after each session ended, and the promise of that was enough to motivate her to keep on getting up early and putting herself through it.

Had she been carrying a bunch of bootcamp enrolment forms in her bag, every person she told this story to would have signed up on the spot. There was something so compelling about the energy with which she talked about it.

She participated in bootcamp because of the incredible high she got afterwards. It's a great example of working towards a thing you want rather than away from something you don't. It's also a lesson in emotional selling - on hearing her describe her experience using emotionally strong and resonant words, others wanted to take part too. And bootcamp is hard. Really hard.

If it was easy, then the experience, the story and the emotional highs wouldn't have been the same.

"I can't tell you how amazing I feel at 7am!"

BOOTCAMP

How do YOU want to feel at 7 am every day?

Customer service excellence

The following factors are top of the list of things people say make them feel good about a service:

- [ ] A smile
- [ ] Feeling heard
- [ ] Feeling important
- [ ] Feeling human
- [ ] Receiving sincere praise

How can you leverage these factors to give great positive customer service?

Long distance runners don't just endure the physical exertion of their challlenge, but also the many psychological games they play to motivate themselves through the distance. Then, once it's all over, they experience a euphoria so great that all the suffering that got them there instantly becomes a thing of the past.

Do you know when the best time is to sign someone up for their next marathon, or 10km race, or Park Run, or triathlon, or workout, or college course, or another difficult and demanding challenge? It's immediately after they have finished the last one, when they are experiencing that buzz moment and they feel utterly invincible. Nothing gives us more confidence to want to achieve something difficult than the experience of success.

Does the service you offer give your customers the opportunity to experience a buzz moment? Can you recognise their efforts and achievements? Can you help them celebrate their great moments? Can you be right there in that buzz moment to let them sign up to their next big challenge?

When is the buzz moment for your customers?

"I've a feeling I've been here, done this, heard this, seen this thing before…"

Usually, it takes several repetitions of a message, a song or an exposure to a brand or a business for us to become aware of it. The simpler the message, the catchier the jingle, the faster it happens.

Getting to that level of awareness was easier in years gone by. There were only a few channels available to communicate with consumers. Purchasing air time or print space in just a small number of commercial TV channels, radio stations and magazines was all it took. Soon, everyone knew who you were. Now, the number of available channels is off the scale, and consumers are finding ways to avoid marketing messages, making the landscape more difficult for brands to expose customers to the required level of repetition.

There is a psychological effect called the "mere-exposure effect"[16]. It's a bias we have towards the things we are already familiar with. We have an instinctive preference for and feel more positive about experiences, brands, music, people and products we already know.

Think about when you hear a song for the first time. When it's new, you don't know what to expect. It takes hearing it

a couple more times to be able to recognise the intro and a few more listens before you find yourself singing along.

The Eurovision Song Contest is one of Europe's more bizarre annual events. The number of countries involved in this contest has dramatically increased since it started in the 1950s, largely to do with the changing geographical and political European landscape. It's grown in size so much that the contest now has to be arranged into semi-final heats, before the winners of those progress to the grand final.

Over 40 nations participate, and most competitors sing in one of two semi-finals, with the winners singing again at the grand final. Six nations get a pass straight to the final. They are the host nation, plus the "big five"- five European nations (France, Germany, Italy, Spain and the UK) who contribute the most financially to the European Broadcasting Union for the running of the contest.

You'd expect this to be an advantage, because it removes the risk of getting bumped out at the earlier stage, but think about it through the lens of exposure and you realise it may actually be a disadvantage.

Currently, 50% of the final score comes from a public vote within each participating country. Simply put, if you want to win, you don't just need a well constructed song, you also need spark, and personality and likeability, and a story. You need to win the hearts of the people of Europe.

By the time of the grand final, the voting public have already heard all the acts that came from the semi-finals, decided which of them they liked, and have probably spent a day or two casually humming their melodies. In contrast, the acts of the host nation and the big five are brand new on the night of the final. There is no familiarity, no connection, no prior exposure.

We can't sing along. We don't know the tune.

Since the rule allowing the big five came into play over 20 years ago, only Germany has won the contest (in 2010), and all but Italy have finished last at least once. Getting a pass to the final isn't an advantage after all. It's actually a lack of critical exposure.

How can you use the exposure effect?

Be consistent. Have a consistent voice, brand elements, colour scheme and visual style across everything.

- ☐ Use consistent language and signage.

- ☐ Provide consistent and high-quality training to your teams so that everyone is aligned with the brand message.

- ☐ Use consistent layout of physical space so customers 'feel' they have visited before, even if they haven't.

☐ ## Show your work early!

Don't wait for the big reveal to introduce your products to customers (or colleagues) for the first time. Share early drafts and talk about what you are doing while you make it.

It all adds up so that customers feel they are somewhere familiar, knowing what to expect and feeling more positive about your products or service.

Do you give your customers a choice as to how they access and use your service? Or are you prescriptive and insist that everyone experiences the same journey?

Research into happiness shows that people feel more positively towards products and services if they have more control and choice over them, and if they are personalised to their specific needs and preferences.

Even if the nature of your service means you are limited in the amount of choice you can offer, can you think of any small details customers can choose, add a preference or personalise? (See examples on pages 138 and 139.)

Choose any colour, as long as it's blue

Stick... or switch

Help customers capture a sensory memory

Choosing the right dress is a special and important part of the wedding experience. A bride-to-be excitedly took her mother to a bridal store to show her three dresses she had shortlisted to choose from. The bride came out in each new dress in turn, only to be told what her mother didn't like about each of them. "Darling, what about the dresses you didn't shortlist?" asked the mother!

Without realising she was doing it, the bride's mother had been playing "stick or switch". She had taken each option as it came, and in the comfort of knowing there were more yet to look at, she had opted to "switch" and focused on what she didn't like about each one. Switch.

The problem with focusing on what you don't like is obvious – it damages what you feel about your choice. You end up feeling like you are choosing between a bad bunch.

Imagine your customers have to make a choice between a number of options, and it is your role to help them choose well. Here are some suggestions to avoid them playing "stick or switch" with you too:

- Lay out all the options at once.

- Or at least say how many options there are at the beginning.

- Demonstrate, describe or talk through all the options first, without judgement or persuasion, before you start to weigh up each one. Ask them to wait until they have seen all available options before they get to share out loud what they are thinking.

- Encourage customers to say out loud what they do like about each option before they say what they find unappealing.

In the wedding dress example there is the added problem that there were three dresses and only one bride. She couldn't try all the dresses on at once. The sensory experience of how it felt to be in each dress became clouded and compromised by the sensation of the next dress, and so on. Have you ever been shopping for a new item of clothing and tried an item on in store, then tried on another item, taken it off and tried on the first one again? Because you wanted to be reminded what the first item felt like? It's the same when you are flat-hunting, or test-driving new cars. We lose that sensory memory.

Sensations and emotions are a significant part of the buying decision, so can you help customers capture a sensory memory for each of their options? Observe their initial reaction. Record what they look like. What they say. The language they use. Their description of how the product made them feel.

Starbucks can make over 80,000 different drinks!

You can see how it would arrive at a number like that. Each of the customisable options multiplies out the possible combinations. You can have americano, espresso, cappuccino, mocha, latte… choose a single shot, double or even a triple (if you really need a caffeine hit). There's regular blend, seasonal blend, single origin specials. Choose between skimmed (non-fat), semi-skimmed (half-fat) or whole (full fat) milk, sugar or sugar-free sweetener, regular temperature or extra hot, or iced, then add one of many types of syrups…. That's before you choose your drink size.

It may be able to serve more than 80,000 combinations of preferences, but in practice, orders will have a long tail and most will probably be from a narrower range of 15-20 more standard requests. Even if most customers choose from the same few drinks it doesn't take away the fact that at Starbucks, each and every customer can have their coffee exactly how they like it.

US mattress manufacturer Helix Sleep invites customers to discover their "sleep DNA" through an online quiz[17] to determine the best mattress configuration for them and whoever they share their bed with. It takes into account factors such as customer height and weight, whether they are side, back or front sleepers, their desired mattress firmness and whether or not they experience back pain. Similar to Starbucks, it takes a baseline of mattress design 'ingredients' and enables them to be configured based on what it believes will be the best match for customers' individual needs. (It also offers a 100-night guarantee and free delivery and returns so you can be confident you are making the right purchase.)

Is your product or service the same for every customer? Is there some way you can customise it based on their preferences and individual needs? As you can see from these examples, many levels of personalisation can be achieved with even a small adjustment across a range of factors.

For customers, having even some level of personalisation creates a feeling of being seen, heard and valued, even if the adjustment is small. It also makes customers feel a greater level of personal ownership of the product or service they bought from you, as if somehow they contributed to the making of it. If you bought a customised Helix mattress based on your personal needs, you'll be more invested in having a great night sleep on it.

It's like a bit of your soul went into making it

When customers booked tickets online on one of Virgin Trains' West Coast Mainline routes, they were asked the reason for their journey. Options included work, school, visiting friends and family, holiday, day out and a final, cheeky "that's for me to know" option. It claimed having this information enabled it to tailor customers' journeys, but every journey for all customers was always exactly the same, regardless of what answer they gave.

Don't fake it

Imagine you are in a busy street and you realise everyone is looking upwards. What do you do? It would take a particularly resistant, willful person not to also look up because we find it instinctive to follow the gaze of others.

Humans have very large and distinctive sclera, the white areas in our eyes that surround our pupils, a feature that allows us to establish from quite a distance where the gaze of another person is directed. It's a nod to our social and collaborative nature and a factor in our excellent ability to judge other people's intentions from their body language. If many other people in the street are looking upwards then there must be something there worth looking at.

Human behaviour leads us to hunt for clues that the things we are choosing to invest our time, resources and effort in are the right things. As complex, social beings, we take a lot of our cues from the actions of others. The rule of thumb goes... "if other people like it, it can't be bad. If lots of other people like it, it must be good."

Therefore, if you can prove to potential customers that many other people choose your products and services, you will raise their appeal.

British people are excellent at waiting in line. If you are British, you will probably at some time have been in a queue without knowing what it was even for - and you know you daren't leave your spot to ask or you'll get bumped to the back of the line. We melt into a puddle of anxiety if we think for a second we might be in the wrong queue, prompting one of those rare occasions where it's considered perfectly acceptable to talk to a total stranger, just to make sure you're in the right place.

With queuing, the rule of thumb goes... "if other people want to do it enough to queue for it, then it must be good."

Studies of queuing behaviour show that people are prepared to stay longer in a slow-moving queue as the number of people behind them also grows. If we are the last in a line and no one else stands behind us, we are more likely to abandon a slow-moving queue[18]. The more people who are behind us, the more we see it as a reinforcement of our decision to stay in line, and the greater the penalty of abandoning our place and having to go back to the start again.

...it must be worth having

140

Review sites like TripAdvisor and Google Maps lever the mechanism of social behaviour to give us an idea of what hotels, restaurants, attractions, and destinations other people are enjoying. Amazon has a "4-star store" in New York City - an actual bricks-and-mortar store that only sells items with an average customer rating of four stars or above.

Hotel comparison sites tell you how many people just booked the hotel you are looking at and how full the town or city is for the dates you have given. Airlines frequently tell you when remaining places are scarce... "only 2 seats left on your chosen date" - a sign you need to hurry and book or be left behind!

These are all systems that make demand visible.

How can you use social cues to raise the desirability of what you offer?

☐ If you have a large customer base, find a way to let potential customers know how many other people choose you (within data protection law, of course!)

☐ Keep customers informed of their place on your waiting lists and how long it will take to get to the front. Consider how you can let them know if many people are behind them on the list.

☐ Share more customer testimonials so that people know others enjoyed your products and service too.

☐ Embrace sites that allow public customer reviews and comments and encourage your customers to leave reviews.

☐ Tell customers when demand is high, when your products and services are close to selling out and when you are at capacity (but be honest).

4 seats left at this price

Value fare

£27.99

TRENDING X
8 customers added to basket in the last 24 hours

POPULAR X
11 customers are viewing this right now

Only 4 in stock online

Add to your basket

Imagine you are out walking through your neighbourhood early one morning, while it's still quiet and there aren't many people about, and you pass another person in the street. Chances are you'll say hello to them, because you somehow belong to the very exclusive "we are people who are up and out early" club. A short while later, when the rest of the world has caught up and the pavements are full of people going about their day, it magically stops. You are no longer in an exclusive club, and the in-group no longer works.

Cyclists do this. Walkers do it too. So do mums with buggies. Train drivers and bus drivers flash their lights and wave as they pass each other. Vintage mini drivers will hop into a convoy on the highway for a couple of miles – just because. Think of the many wonderful and varied types of associations, owner's clubs and fan groups who spend time together because they all like the same thing.

Humans have an extra liking for others with whom we share a key common thing: people in a recognisable in-group with us. It's called the "in-group bias"[19], an unconscious attraction towards others in a group we also belong to. It goes something like this… they like the same thing I do… they have similar values to me… they are similar to me… I like them more.

It works for invisible things too, which you can only uncover from conversation, like having the same name (or even the same first initial), the same star sign, the same life experiences and liking the same holiday destination.

Any way you can show customers that you are human too, that you live lives like they do, that you struggle with the same daily things they do, that you like the same things they do, the in-group strengthens and customers will like you more.

People buy from and are more persuaded by people they like and who are like them. In what ways are you like your customers? Authentically. And how can you demonstrate it?

In what ways are you like your customers?

The opposite is true. Any time HR makes an announcement that badly affects the workforce, any time a company unfairly changes the T&Cs on their customers, any time a company wields its power unreasonably over an individual, they demonstrate the opposite of the in-group. An out-group.

When you present a "them and us" position, you create a divide, you damage the connection and the affection for you and your product dims.

Sign value

As high-end yoga apparel company, lululemon, was building its men's range it had a seperate men's store in SoHo, New York, in which it created an in-store service called "The Joinery". Customers could select a pair of shorts and choose their preferred liner and a member of the in-store team would machine stitch them together for them while they waited. A personalised choice and a personalised pair of shorts. These shorts were unique in that they carried a small red version of the company logo on them, a feature you couldn't get on any other item of clothing in any of their other stores.

Even though customers could buy a pair of pre-lined shorts they still chose to have them machined in store, because the shorts with the red logo were already gaining attention in New York's gyms and fitness studios and customers wanted them.

These logos were very small, just a few millimeters in diameter. A tiny detail, the smallest difference, but they had sign value. Sign value is a small detail that only someone from an insider group could recognise. Perhaps the mark of a genuine luxury brand, a detail on a vintage watch, a small feature on a product that nods to a special edition.

Create an insider group for your customers by creating a distinctive small detail in your products that only they will recognise, so they can feel they belong to something unique and a bit special.

Create a distinctive, small detail, only customers will recognise

Shhhhh....

We all love to be in on a secret, don't we. Inspired by the Prohibition Era in the USA, Evans and Peel Detective Agency is a cocktail bar in West London with no remarkable street presence - just a plain door with a buzzer. You step inside to a vintage detective agency where you have to share a compelling story of a mystery it needs to help you solve. It's worth preparing a fun story.

If it's a good enough story then you're in! Behind a bookcase is the secret entrance to a fantastic cocktail bar. You're welcome.

Rise to the challenge!

Children in Need, Sport Relief, Stoptober, Movember, Race for Life and World's Biggest Coffee Morning are just some of a long list of huge-scale events that we challenge ourselves to participate in; events where we get to feel part of a large movement.

Events with big meaning

We are motivated by the idea of joining up with other people to achieve something we couldn't do alone. Can you create a project at scale, a community challenge, or a group effort that will make people want to contribute and take part?

In March 2019, severe cold weather created difficult flying conditions and low visability across much of Europe. Amsterdam Schiphol airport, Europe's busiest airport, was operating at reduced capacity while greater distance was maintained between aircraft taking off and landing. Flights were delayed across Europe and beyond because they needed the certainty of a landing time before they could set off.

Passengers awaiting a KLM flight from Manchester to Amsterdam were disappointed to discover their flight would be at least four hours late. But this was no ordinary announcement. Instead of the message coming from one of the airport gate staff in the usual polite but impersonal manner, a tall, impeccably dressed gentleman wearing a uniform with four stripes and a flat hat with braiding emerged from the gate and took the microphone. He introduced himself as the flight's captain, explained the situation and the reason for the delay, promised passengers his priority was their collective safety and said he would stay at the gate for the next hour to talk to anyone who had any questions for him.

It was instantly disarming, and, true to his word, he stayed, talked, answered questions, alleviated anxieties and relayed updates. It was a rare personal touch in an environment that is becoming less and less human and more focused on security and operational efficiency.

For the simple joy of it

Gamification has become a somewhat overused phrase, unfortunately consigned by many as a passing trend in management jargon. But the principles behind it have barely been exploited, and are a largely untapped and powerful way of generating happy and pleasantly-surprised customers.

Gamification is the process of using game mechanics and elements of games, such as chance, leaderboards, trades, surprise, prizes and rewards, to make an interaction with a product or service a delight for its own sake.

thefuntheory.com, created by Volkswagen, highlights innovative ways people have used game mechanics to bring joy to simple things like recycling, driving safely and walking up stairs.

Can you engineer some surprise fun into what you do? Don't tell customers in advance... the suprise is half of the delight!

LEADERBOARD

1	James	204
2	Alan	176
3	Michael	127
4	Deborah	96
5	Katherine	91
6	Wes	88
7	Vikki	72
8	Annette	61
9	Erica	48
10	Tom	45
11	Sara	26
12	Shivali	14

Game elements, such as leaderboards and scores, can add to customer motivation.

During the build up to the 2014 Sochi Winter Olympics, passengers on the Moscow Metro were offered a free ride if they completed 30 standing squats. Transport officials installed ticket machines that could track and count up the number of squats passengers completed and issue free tickets to those who reached 30.

In 2010, Nike introduced an augmented game called "The Grid" to encourage people to run the streets of London.

Tracked by 'checking in' at specially branded public telephone boxes, runners competed for points and awards, comparing their progress on leaderboards and boosting their scores with difficult, early, late or group runs.

Make the game elements *Random*

Coffee chain Pret A Manger uses the variable reward of an occasional random free coffee to brighten the day of its customers. Team members can give a free coffee to any customer they want to, entirely at their own discretion and with no rules and guidelines about to whom or why. They can choose any customer if they think it will make their day. It's a great way to make customers smile.

It's been proven that variable rewards adjust our behaviour more than predictable ones. Not knowing the outcome of our actions is one of the reasons we are hooked on smartphone apps, computer games, and social media products. We keep on scrolling, in case something really great, like a cute cat video, is hiding just out of sight.

Our memories of past experiences are stored as mental 'polaroids' of significant moments

When we think back to a past experience, positive or negative, we don't think of the sum of the total experience. Instead, we get the essence of the memory in the form of mental snapshots, usually shaped by both the most intense moment of the experience and also the way the experience ended.

Imagine you could go on the trip of a lifetime, the most amazing experience ever, but the catch is that you can't remember it afterwards?

This question is posed by Daniel Kahnemann in *"Thinking Fast and Slow"*[20]. He raises the question of what an experience is. Is it the experience itself or is it the memory it generates for us to reflect upon and share afterwards?

There are two of us going through life

There's the version of us who experiences our life, and the version of us who remembers it.

He concludes that there are essentially two of each of us going through life. There's the version of us who experiences our life, and the version of us who remembers it.

We don't remember in real time. If you think back to your last holiday, you won't start that memory from the beginning, with the moment you closed the front door of your home and set off on your travels.

It's more likely you'll have instantly gone to the key moments of the holiday. What the pool looked like. How the cold wind felt while you were on that coastal walk. That incredible meal you had on your second night there. It's not just the great parts either, you'll remember the bad stuff such as the rude greeting you got at reception, the leak in the bathroom, the flight delay at the airport and the bad fall or case of food poisoning you had.

It's the significant moments we remember. The peaks (highs) or the troughs (lows). We store them as kind of mental 'polaroids', never the full technicolour version, but enough to smile (or wince) at the memory.

Even if a trip was almost all good, one particularly awful moment of it will be enough to make that the thing we recall when we think back to it.

As well as the significant moments, we also store in our memories the feeling of how an experience ended.

This is called the "peak-end rule"[21], and studies have shown this is how we consistently commit experiences to memory, regardless of their duration. It's as if there are constantly two versions of ourselves operating in parallel, one of us living in the moment and experiencing things in the here and now,

and another one of us that stores away the snapshots of what we just did to our memory.

If you want customers to have an amazing experience with you, pay attention to the tiny details through the whole length of the customer journey (the experiencing self). If you want customers to remember their amazing experience with you, so much that they head home and rave to their friends and family about how incredible you are (the remembering self) then you need to create exceptional peaks and pay attention to how the experience ends. The more memorable the experience of your service, the more your customers will talk and share their stories with others.

"We are the sum of all the moments in our lives."

Thomas Wolfe

(Well, the moments our remembering self chooses to store!)

Actually, there's three of us...

Mindfulosophy space in lululemon's flagship store on 5th Avenue, NYC
June 2018

There's another version of us choosing what we want to share with others

As well as the version of ourselves doing life and the version of ourselves taking those personal mental polaroid snapshots of our key memories, there's a third version of us, walking behind the other two, looking through the polaroids, sifting out only the best ones, the best angles and the most iconic spaces, dusting them down, adding a filter or two and uploading them to social media platforms, like Instagram, to share with others.

Flagship stores everywhere are becoming less about the sales per square foot, and more about creating iconic and beautiful spaces, "Instagrammable spaces", that simply demand to be photographed and shared. Those seeking their own source of social media love, likes, shares and comments will gravitate towards the best of them to capture the same images for their own online showreels.

THE EXPERIENCING
SELF

THE REMEMBERING
SELF

THE SHARING
SELF

One of the best indicators of brand loyalty is brand memory. In order to enjoy an engaging and enduring positive relationship with customers, your products or services first need to be easy to recall.

If you can show up in the memories of your customers (for all the right reasons, of course), you will have taken the first step to generating a loyal customer base. What better way to create a lasting memory with customers than to have them lock in those memories in the moment with a photograph they share with others.

Our social brains are hardwired to make us want to do things that draw approval from others, and we are rewarded by a small hit of dopamine every time we succeed. This instinct was created to enable real deep social connections and cooperation between ourselves and others, but we find the pleasurable effects of dopamine so addictive we have short-circuited the reward system and we get the same small rush from any approval we get from others on social media. Of course, our brains evolved this feature long before the invention of social media, but this instinct of ours is one of the reasons for the wild success of the medium.

Every like, heart, share, retweet, comment or other engagement that we receive on social media gives us the same small dopamine hit. Quite literally, getting a positive response from other people about a tweet, a Facebook update or an Instagram picture makes us happy for a moment.

The problem is, so many people are sharing stories and uploading content online that most social media has just become noise. To generate any significant amount of attention (and the dopamine rush that comes with it), users now have to come up with something particularly eye-catching or particularly emotionally resonant.

If you can create a beautiful environment, customers will want to visit and photograph it. If you create a great customer experience, customers will want to tell people about it. You will be doing both yourself and your customers a favour. You get to be talked about in a positive way, great for brand recognition, and they get socially rewarded with a shot of dopamine.

Page 74 describes the gift shops visitors to Disney parks walk through after each ride they experience. The products on sale in each one differs depending on the story and characters of the ride itself, but they all perform the same function – your ability to buy an artefact to cement the memory of the experience you just had.

Souvenirs are physical mementos that people buy and give that connect them to particular memories. The word souvenir is French and literally means "remembrance" or "memory". We pepper our lives with items we have collected from our travels, gifts from friends, pieces we have assembled, each of which connect us to a moment in our past, which contributes to the story we tell ourselves of who we are.

The tiny salt and pepper pots distributed during meal service on Virgin Atlantic flights are designed to be "stealable" so passengers can take away a small positive memory of their flight with them. It's the same with the cotton coasters provided at the Bassoon Bar in London's Corinthia Hotel - far too cool to leave behind.

♥ London

What memento can you encourage your customers to buy (or take) to remind them of their experience with you?

"*What We Keep*", by authors Bill Shapiro and Naomi Wax[22], is a collection of stories about people (many of them famous) and their single-most treasured possession. You might expect this book to detail a series of highly prized, glittering and expensive items, but it does the opposite. The items we value most often have the least monetary value, but they are things that help us tell a story about who we are, the people we care about the most and the moments that shaped our lives.

Experiencing something truly transformational creates strong memories. Those memories will be strengthened further by a physical artefact, a souvenir, which will act as an occasional reminder of the experience, and a source of inspiration to share the story with others.

"On a scale of 0-10, how likely are you to recommend _____ to a friend or colleague?"

your product or service

| 0 | 1 | 2 | 3 | 4 | 5 | 6 | 7 | 8 | 9 | 10 |

DETRACTORS   PASSIVES   PROMOTERS

NPS® = (% PROMOTERS) - (% DETRACTORS)

Also known as the 'friends and family test', the Net Promoter Score®[23] is a metric that attempts to quantify a subjective experience. Customers are asked if the experience is memorable enough that they would consider mentioning it to someone else, hopefully in a positive way. It's a blunt instrument, but it will give you clues as to whether your customers remember you for the right reasons and gives you chance to monitor changes if you experiment with improving the experience for them.

The score is based on the fact we all love to give a recommendation. Recommendations carry social currency. If we can help solve a problem for another person by helping them find a trusted service and they have a good experience of it, then it looks good on us. It paints us as a person in-the-know and it validates our own decision to have used that service too.

At an individual customer level, a score of six or less means you missed the mark so far that they will be telling their friends all the bad things about their experience. A seven or eight puts you in the category of simply meeting expectations. If all you did was deliver on what was expected of you then you aren't talk-worthy. However, do something unqiue and exhiliarating for customers, which goes above and beyond their expectations, and you'll be hitting those nines and tens.

An overall NPS above zero (using the formula above) means more customers are positively raving about you than are complaining about you.

Surprise and delight customers and you may have just given them a topic to share with their friends next time they get together. Their story about your product or service will be competing with all the other catch-up gossip, but if it is unique, positive and different enough, it will find itself in the conversation. The person sharing will want their experience validating by their friends so they will share all the best bits, in excited and persuasive tones, and will be delighted if one of their friends chooses to try it too. (You'll be delighted too.)

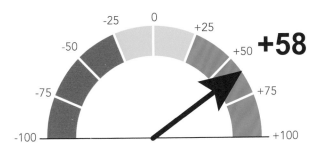

I won because...

I believed more, I trained harder, I wanted it more...

I passed my exam because... I studied hard, I prepared well, I'm intelligent...

I succeeded in life and business because... I got up early, I tried harder, I worked smarter, I was more disciplined...

After the Olympic final the winner predictably is asked why they won. We ask CEOs of large corporations for the secrets of their success. They all tell us about how they tried and they trained and they applied themselves, and, most of all, how much they believed in themselves. The thing is, so did the athlete who finished seventh. So did the entrepreneur who didn't secure the investment. When we ask the winner how they did what they did, what we hear reflected back to us is their personal belief about the factors that led to their achievement. But it's skewed, attributing successes more to positive, internal, personal traits than fortunate external events.

There's a flip side to this narrative - we also have a habit of attributing our failures and our losses to external factors.

- The student who failed an exam may say they failed because the lecturer hadn't covered the whole syllabus in class, there was a lot of distracting noise outside the exam hall, or they hadn't slept well the night before.

- The entrepreneur who didn't succeed may say bad weather slowed down their sales, their website crashed on a key trading day, and the person who was meant to listen to their investment pitch was 15 minutes late and distracted when they arrived.

- The athlete may say they didn't win because the opposition had better equipment, they were recovering from injury, or a noise from the crowd meant they missed a critical shot.

It's not a conscious process - it's the result of a subconscious bias called the "self-serving bias"[24], which protects the ego of the individual to allow them a more positive outlook on life.

Who wants to believe they didn't achieve their biggest life goals because they lacked vision, motivation and talent?

It's a particular thing in western countries with a greater culture of individualism, where people are conditioned to believe that anything in the world is possible if we just want it enough. We just have to want it more than the next person.

How does the self-serving bias impact you?

1 Someone might say the reason they didn't achieve what they wanted is because of your organisation, service or product. They may say they didn't succeed because your delivery was a day late, your product was ill-fitting and they didn't get the confirmation email you sent. This is potentially a lose-lose situation for you, because if you argue that the customer was solely to blame for their misfortune, you hurt their ego - not exactly a way to win affection either.

2 When you conduct research with customers, you might not get the whole story when asking them to describe past actions, pain points and what they think they need.

3 When you read a business biography, or watch an interview with a winning sportsperson describing how they became successful, they will probably miss out one of the key factors - some of it was luck.

When you celebrate your own success, enjoy the moment, but also see point 3 above.

Seen through the eyes of others...

Nothing boosts our mood more than receiving genuine and positive praise from someone who's opinion we value. You can make someone's day right now by telling them something that you really like about them - what trait they have that you admire. Maybe they always turn up to meetings prepared. Perhaps they are always upbeat and positive in their outlook. Maybe they always have a logical, balanced opinion. It could be that you admire their honesty, or their fantastic sense of style. Whatever it is, make sure it's authentic.

As well as making us feel good in the moment, receiving authentic praise gives us a positive reputation to live up to. If someone tells us they admire the way we deal with customers' problems, we are likely to want to continue to serve customers to the best of our ability.

Give others a great reputation they will want to live up to

Dirty Knowledge!

Is there a song you know all the lyrics to, a movie you have watched over and over, a silly dance you have all the moves to… but you don't want other people to know? Maybe there's a TV programme your friends all agree is terrible, but it's your secret 'guilty pleasure' and you enjoy watching it. You won't be in a rush to divulge you know the characters and the latest storyline. We all have what we call 'dirty knowledge' - a light term for information we keep to ourselves to protect our reputation so the people around us don't think of us differently.

In the world of economics, "free" is a little bit magical. The idea of getting something for nothing appeals to the very basic of human drivers. If we purchase products based on the balance of how big the benefit we expect from the item is compared to the amount it will cost us, then to have any benefit at all divided by "free" (or zero) means that economically speaking, we would always choose a free option. If you were offered a free product you liked, with no strings attached, you'd most likely take it. If you buy goods online, free delivery beats paying for delivery every time, as long as the product price remains the same.

However, free does sometimes get us into trouble. We buy things we don't need because we are attracted to buy-one-get-one-free offers. We try free samples because they are free, but then we feel awkwardly obliged to buy the product. Sometimes, we are blinded by a free offer and then miss out on an alternative that would have suited us better. Free works well if it is easy to accept. Imagine you were offered a free chocolate bar, but you had to visit a venue three miles away - would you go to the trouble of collecting it?

Who doesn't want free chocolate?

FREE DELIVERY

'Free' can be an excellent mechanism to attract the initial attention of customers

but... free has a downside

During the planning of services, organisations can be guilty of "barrier-bashing"; that is, creating a list of why they think customers don't access services and then try to solve each one in turn. They may make it free to attend, throw in childcare and free transport, arrange for it to be held near customers' homes, provide any necessary equipment, and give a free cuppa for good measure. The problem is that they become so busy trying to make it more accessible that they can end up giving the impression that it's not worth anything.

When it comes to services, "free" can come with hidden subtext that says "this is a little bit rubbish". If it's free, then it has no value. If customers are used to paying £5 for a fitness class and then get offered one for free, they can jump to the very wrong conclusion that it will be many times lower standard than the class they could have paid for, even if it is with the same instructor and at the same venue.

The customer thinks: "They can't even give this thing away. It mustn't be that good."

There's another factor at play too - consumer power. Paying for services gives customers a certain sense of power. If they are receiving stuff for free, they may feel like they have to be passive recipients, who should just be grateful for what they get - they lose some of their voice and don't get to call the shots.

Do you offer any free services? If you do, can you put a charge on them instead? If you believe that adding a fee means you won't be able to compete with rival brands or services, then in what way can you raise the quality and style with which you deliver?

It can't be that good!

Every 'purchase' you make has a cost/benefit exchange and the point at which you make a decision to buy is the point at which you believe the expected benefits of doing so, will exceed the expected costs (at least in that moment). It's easy to think of the costs in just money terms, but that would be a mistake, because costs also include the time and effort you put in.

Netflix's CEO, Reed Hastings, famously said its greatest competition came from sleep! - a nod to the addictive nature of binge-watching TV, and recognition that Netflix isn't just in competition with other TV channels and media sources, but the choice of not watching any TV at all.

Your service costs, therefore, also include the 'opportunity cost' of your customers missing out on all the other things they could choose to use their time and energy on instead, including the option of doing nothing.

While we instinctively recognise the need to reduce customer resistance to participation, it only addresses one side of the equation. That is, we can spend a lot of time making our thing cheap and easy, rather than making it desirable and worthwhile.

It's better if we can present the case to our target audiences that the expected benefits are so overwhelmingly wonderful they will want to turn the earth over to get them. And I mean truly wonderful - actual benefits that real, emotional humans will actually want.

If your product or service is free, talk about how good it is to raise its perceived value. Tell customers what it's worth.

- "Our smoke-free service is so successful, and delivered by our exceptional and highly experienced team. It costs us £240 for each person we support, but we care about your health and we don't want the cost to be a barrier for you, so we're offering it to you for free."

- "We're so confident you'll love how great you feel on our fitness programme, that the first month is on us."

- "You bring your motivation, we'll provide the rest."

If it's free, tell people what it's worth

"This industry-leading course normally costs £180 per person, but we want you to enjoy it, and the opportunities it will bring you, so we made it free for you, but only if you commit to attending the full three days."

These are money examples. When considering whether or not to 'buy' from you, customers will be looking for a wide range of clues that they are making the right decision. (See section on certainty from page 89.)

Top 10 lists are everywhere. Who knew that pretty much everything you ever needed to know in life about any topic could be boiled down perfectly to ten points? Next time you see a Top 10 list, ask yourself which of the following two categories it falls into...

Category 1 – We had to pick the best ten. There were so many incredible suggestions to choose from but we had to stop at ten to keep it short. It means there are amazing benefits we didn't get round to sharing, but having a nice round number of ten is good, right?

Category 2 – We had to scrape the barrel to get to ten and the last few are garbage! There are three great benefits, three average ones, two more slightly dubious ones and two more that totally scraped the barrel. Just to get to ten. Because ten is an actual thing (apparently).

How about instead... "Here are the top ways in which our service or product will really make a different to your life. Of course there are more, but we stopped at only the really great ones."

Stop at just the really great ones!

empty barrel

Since the 1980s, Vancouver company John Fleuvog Shoes has been carving an unusual route through the world of footwear design. Its unique, bold and unconventional styles have been worn by Madonna, Beyonce, Alice Cooper and Lady Gaga. Fleuvog's first store in Granville Street, Vancouver, was designed to look like an elaborate bedroom - certainly ahead of its time on experiential retail, as 40 years later, a space like that would be highly Instagramable! Tongue-in-cheek slogans such as "No, you're weird" stare back at passers-by looking in from outside.

John Fleuvog Shoes stores can be found in major cities across North America but its community is truly global. Its innovative "Open Source Footwear" programme encourages enthusiasts and budding designers to submit their own unique Fleuvog shoe designs. Uploaded designs are showcased on its website at fleuvog.com, where visitors can vote for their favourites. John Fleuvog himself takes inspiration from these submissions and any designs he uses, he credits the original designer, names the shoe after them and sends them a free pair.

Are you a creative genius, but footwear design isn't your thing?

The "Fleuvog Creative" programme for advertising design operates in a similar way. Customers respond to a creative brief by submitting artwork online, the best of which are used by the company.

Sweets make people happy
And happiness makes us more creative

Being happy apparently makes us more creative. In a study on creative problem-solving, a group of junior doctors were asked to come up with as many causes as possible of a hypothetical set of symptoms in patients[25]. They were split into two groups, a 'happy' group and a control group. The 'happy' group came up with more possible causes in much less time than the control group.

How did they get to be happy? They were given sweets.

But they didn't get to eat them! The study team didn't want the effect of sugar to cloud the results, so participants were given sweets to eat later, and their elevated level of happiness was still enough to generate a significant improvement in creative problem-solving .

Fast-casual Italian restaurant chain Vapiano offer customers a small handful of Haribo jelly teddy bears as they leave – a sure way to make the last moment of their dining experience a positive one.

- Check your headline message. Is it positive? If not, can you make it positive?

- What changes would make your service "every customer's dream"?

- How can you make your product or service more fun? (Without over-engineering it.)

- When is the buzz moment for your customers? People are more likely to commit to further engagement when they are experiencing the "buzz!" (For example, marathon runners signing up for their next challenge on the finish line of their last one.)

- Can you use game mechanics to find novel and innovative ways to surprise and delight your customers, just for smiles? Applied correctly, gamification not only makes your customers happy, but creates moments and stories that they will share with their friends, driving up your reputation.

- The following are all at the top of the list of things people say make them feel good about a service: a smile, feeling heard, feeling important, feeling human. How can you leverage those factors to give great positive customer service?

- Does your service or product offer opportunities for customers to connect and socialise with others?

- Can you find a way to demonstrate to customers how many other people love your product or service? We take cues from other people to check the things we want are like the things other people want. Visible demand offers reassurance.

Can you demonstrate to customers that you and your team are actually just like them? People are more drawn to people who are like themselves. Show them you too are dog-loving, coffee-loving, red car driving, stationery nerds…

Can you create a subtle, visible sign in your products that only those in the know will recognise, so they will feel part of an in-group?

People feel happier when they have more control over a situation. Is your service or product prescriptive, or do customers have choice and control over how they access it?

Do customers have a number of options to choose from? If so, lay out all the options at once before you discuss the various merits of them. This will stop them looking for the faults in each option because they will know there are no more to choose from. Otherwise, they may get to the last possible option and not like it, and have discounted all the alternatives already.

How people see you is important. Take a walk through your service with an open mind. What do you notice? Is it positive?

People love to rise to a challenge with 'big meaning'. They are motivated by joining up with other people to achieve something bigger than they could manage on their own. Children in Need, Sport Relief, Race for Life… can you create a project at scale that will encourage people to take part?

Bright colours (especially yellow) are associated with being positive. Check your colour palette.

Think of a highly positive brand. Imagine someone from their team gave you some tips on how to generate smiles from your customers. What might they tell you?

QUESTIONS

☐ Providing your service for free may seem like a good idea to increase take-up, but it can de-value what you offer. If your service is free, can you emphasise what it is worth and how beneficial it will be for customers, so it retains its value?

☐ What do you want your customers to remember? Can you create particularly positive moments where you especially delight them?

☐ Can you provide extra support and reassurance at their most difficult times? And can you think of ways of making the end of each interaction your customers have with you particularly positive and memorable?

☐ Can you enable customers to share their experience and memory? Do you have an "Instagramable" backdrop they will want to photograph? Can they immerse themselves in your brand in a way that they will be eager to share online and with friends? Each heart, like, share and retweet they get will make them happy and give your reputation a boost!

☐ Do you have a long list of positive benefits for customers using your product or service? If so, don't share all of them. Stop at only the really good ones.

☐ Can you share your work early? Demonstrate an early prototype, talk about your product or service in the making, encourage people to try the beta version. Simply being exposed to something a number of times makes it seem more familiar and customers will feel more positively towards it.

☐ Can you personalise your product or service so it's even more perfect for customers? Starbucks and Helix Sleep have a core offer that can be tailored so customers can have their products exactly how they like them.

☐ What artefacts or souvenirs can customers take to help them remember their experience with you?

☐ Reminder: Sweets make people happy!

Simplified

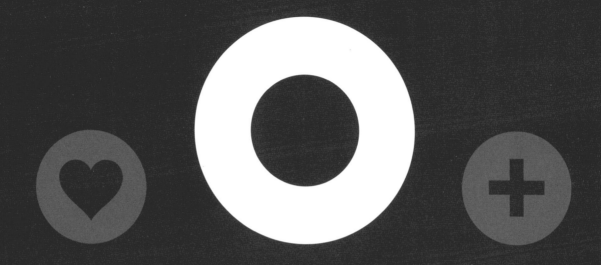

To really engage with customers, services need to be desirable... and easy to access

Desirable

Frustration

If your service is desirable and people want it, but they find it hard to access and use it, they will become frustrated and may give up.

Engagement

Having engaged customers requires having a service that people want, and making it easy for them to access and use that service.

Easy

Disinterest

Even if your business case shows that there is a need for your service, if you design one that is difficult to access and don't present it in an appealing way, customers won't come.

Apathy

If your service doesn't seem appealing enough, then regardless of how easy it is to access and use, customers won't be motivated enough to fully engage with you.

The first four themes of Desire Code are concerned with making a service as desirable as possible, more "wantable", to raise its demand and keep customer motivation high. This principle works alongside the other four, and it's essential for creating customer engagement and adherence. Quite simply, as well as making it desirable, you need to make it as easy as possible for people to be able to access and use the service you provide.

simplify

Customers may really want your product, but if they are faced with long queues at checkouts, long waits on the phone, too many steps, instructions that are difficult to understand and appointments that are inconvenient, they will quickly lose interest and find an alternative. We've all experienced this. Delivering an excellent customer experience means paying attention to the small details, the things that are easily overlooked, which might just make all the difference to your customers.

if it's hard to use, it wont be used!

Do you want customers to keep hold of information? Make it 'sticky' by connecting it with something useful they will want to keep or enable them to have a digital copy on their smartphones.

Do you give customers physical products to use? Folders or resources? Can you make it easier for people to carry them?

We're here!

If customers visit you in person, how can you make it easier for them to find you? (e.g. give details of where they can park, the name of the nearest bus stop)

Push button
Wait for signal

Pages 8-11 of this book describe how to use insights from customers to map out the journey they experience and to plot an approximate funnel showing where there are significant drop-out points.

Look at your customer journey. Pay particular attention to any steps you have identified that lead to a high drop out, but still consider the whole picture.

At every single step, ask yourself whether it can be made easier for customers.

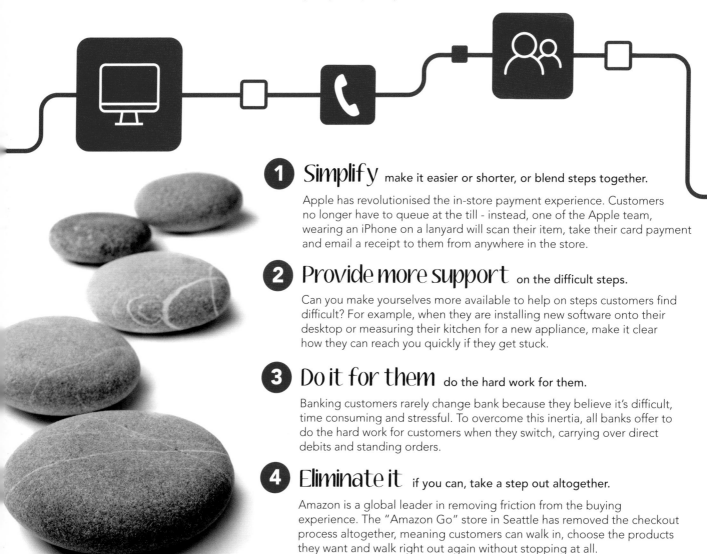

1 Simplify make it easier or shorter, or blend steps together.

Apple has revolutionised the in-store payment experience. Customers no longer have to queue at the till - instead, one of the Apple team, wearing an iPhone on a lanyard will scan their item, take their card payment and email a receipt to them from anywhere in the store.

2 Provide more support on the difficult steps.

Can you make yourselves more available to help on steps customers find difficult? For example, when they are installing new software onto their desktop or measuring their kitchen for a new appliance, make it clear how they can reach you quickly if they get stuck.

3 Do it for them do the hard work for them.

Banking customers rarely change bank because they believe it's difficult, time consuming and stressful. To overcome this inertia, all banks offer to do the hard work for customers when they switch, carrying over direct debits and standing orders.

4 Eliminate it if you can, take a step out altogether.

Amazon is a global leader in removing friction from the buying experience. The "Amazon Go" store in Seattle has removed the checkout process altogether, meaning customers can walk in, choose the products they want and walk right out again without stopping at all.

Your customer base is broader than you think. Even if you serve a relatively small market, such as a service for a particular age group, or within a small town, your customers will be diverse and have diverse needs. They could have one of many physical impairments, or more hidden, sensory ones. They may have a debilitating health condition you know nothing about. They may face discrimination on a daily basis and you may not see it. They may be of a generation that doesn't fully understand what it is you do or have the tools to access it, but they still need it and maybe they need some assistance.

Designing an accessible service should never be an afterthought. For a start, it makes total business sense. If your product or service is inaccessible for groups of your customers, you may find you don't have many customers left. More than that, discrimination is unlawful and if you work in the public sector, the Public Sector Equality Duty[26] spells out the minimum expected of your service. But more than all of that, it's the right thing to do.

Making your product or service accessible to all may mean you have to make certain adjustments to how you design and deliver it, and these adjustments can be harder to add in later on. Far better to bake them in from the start.

Talk to customers with experience of having different needs for using your products and accessing your services. Test your concepts and your prototypes with them. Ask them which steps of your service they struggle with and why. Observe them interacting with your products to identify if there's any part they find hard to use. Have your design team become their biggest advocators.

If you design with the intention of making your product or service accessible for anyone, you will have designed a better one for everyone.

Have you had an experience of driving to a destination in an unfamiliar town or city where you are confidently following road signs, and are almost there, but you suddenly find yourself at a junction with no sign and it's not clear which way to go? Do you go left or right? There's another car impatiently hovering behind you so you have to make a snap choice. You know that if you choose wrong you'll probably end up in the wrong part of town navigating a one-way system.

Don't you hate it when road signs dry up?!

You've probably had a similar experience too when engaging with a brand or service. You think you are waiting for the washing machine repair company to call you back, or was it that you needed to call them? Did the GP say they'd call you with your blood test results, or are you meant to follow up? When did they say they'd have them? It's possible you were told what would happen next as you were leaving your last appointment, but you don't remember.

You've signed up to attend an event, but did you get the ticket yet? Was it coming by post? By email? Did you see the small print that said you must bring it with you? Did you come to the wrong counter or department? Are you sitting in the wrong reception area? The wrong departure gate?

At each step of your customer journey do you explicitly tell customers what the next step is, who will take it, when it will be done by and what to expect? Do you explain exactly where to go, which entrance to use, how to pay, who to ask for, what day or time to be there and what to bring?

If customers are waiting a long time for the next step, do you do anything to reassure them that all is still fine? Perhaps they are waiting several months for a knee operation, for a legal process to complete, for their child to get a place in their local gymnastics club or for a rare item they ordered from abroad to be imported. They could be waiting a while without hearing anything and mistakenly believe something has gone wrong. You may find you and your team are spending more time than you would want fielding enquiries from anxious customers checking that they haven't missed anything and asking for updates.

Check your customer service inbox and talk to those who talk directly to customers. Look for clues to see if there is anywhere that customers are unsure of what the next step is.

Can you make it easier for them by being extra clear at every stage about what happens next? Can you enable them to track progress online or have notifications and reminders sent to them via multiple channels? Can you give them more detailed and specific instructions, or make it possible for them to always deal with the same person?

Be clear about what happens next

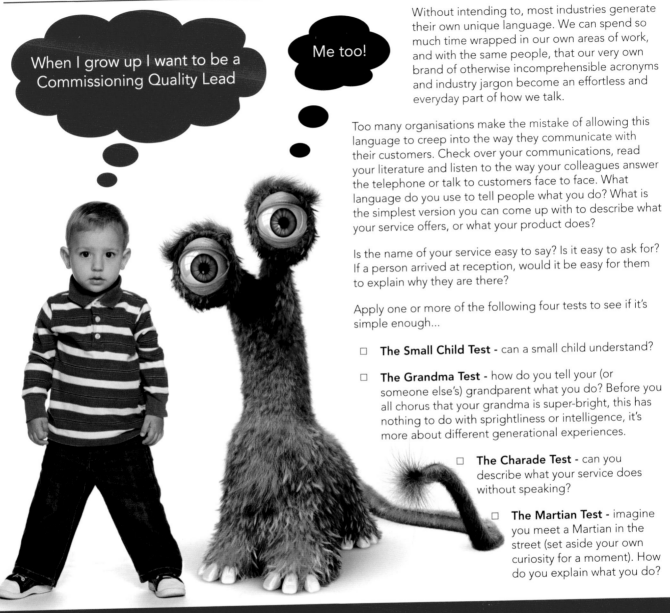

When I grow up I want to be a Commissioning Quality Lead

Me too!

Without intending to, most industries generate their own unique language. We can spend so much time wrapped in our own areas of work, and with the same people, that our very own brand of otherwise incomprehensible acronyms and industry jargon become an effortless and everyday part of how we talk.

Too many organisations make the mistake of allowing this language to creep into the way they communicate with their customers. Check over your communications, read your literature and listen to the way your colleagues answer the telephone or talk to customers face to face. What language do you use to tell people what you do? What is the simplest version you can come up with to describe what your service offers, or what your product does?

Is the name of your service easy to say? Is it easy to ask for? If a person arrived at reception, would it be easy for them to explain why they are there?

Apply one or more of the following four tests to see if it's simple enough...

☐ **The Small Child Test -** can a small child understand?

☐ **The Grandma Test -** how do you tell your (or someone else's) grandparent what you do? Before you all chorus that your grandma is super-bright, this has nothing to do with sprightliness or intelligence, it's more about different generational experiences.

☐ **The Charade Test -** can you describe what your service does without speaking?

☐ **The Martian Test -** imagine you meet a Martian in the street (set aside your own curiosity for a moment). How do you explain what you do?

How do you describe what you do?

Affordance is a characteristic of a product that makes it obvious to the user how they should use and interact with it.

Mobile and tablet devices operated by touch and pinch gestures are a type of affordance. Regardless of their manufacturer or operating system, these devices operate in the same intuitive way. Give a toddler a touch-screen device and they know exactly how to use it. They aren't just mimicking the actions of adults, they are actually using them to play games and watch content.

A pull handle on a door, a button on a pedestrian crossing, a scooter. We don't need to be told how to use these products, we just know.

Playgrounds are built on affordance. A single glance at a slide, a swing or a climbing frame and it's instantly obvious what to do. Children don't need a user manual to play in the park.

Playing cards have a unique hand-feel. Nothing else in the world can create the same physical sensation as holding a deck of playing cards, and we all hold them the same way. Hand a deck of cards to anyone, and you will see that when they are not consciously shuffling or distributing the cards, they will instinctively fidget with them in a predictable manner.

People just know how to hold a deck of cards

Have you ever wondered why the "QWERTY" keyboard design is the global standard used on all computers, laptops and touchscreen devices? The QWERTY key layout was introduced with the manual typewriter and it was designed to minimise the jamming of typebars, those thin metal arms that fling forward and leave the imprint of their letter on the ribbon. Strike two adjacent letters together and the typebars get stuck.

There have been alternative keyboard systems proposed over the years, ones that promised a more efficient typing experience, given we no longer need to worry about jammed-up typewriters. But they have all failed, even if they were superior, because the convention has been set. We are all used to the QWERTY layout; we don't want to re-learn the coordinated action of a new set up, and manufacturers don't want to bet on making one either.

A convention makes it as easy as possible for customers to use

Both conventions and affordance are essential ingredients if you are to produce a product that customers can use "straight out of the box". You are free to ignore these conventions in your own design, but you make it harder for customers to use your products if you do.

Road signs are a designed convention for providing shorthand instructions to road users. They vary a little from nation to nation, but the overall principles are the same, and they follow a set formula in terms of shape, colour and iconography.

The "Transport" typeface used on UK road signs was specially designed to be easy to read at a distance by the drivers of fast-moving vehicles on the motorway. Its easy legibility is the reason it's been adopted as the typeface for the UK Government Digital Service (GDS) design system[27]. All government digital services with a URL ending gov.uk use the same design standard, including the Transport typeface.

User experience design uses conventions to prompt users to know what to do next and how to move around an interface. A website's "Home" page is usually accessed from the top left hand corner of the screen. Log in/log out and account information is usually found on the top right. Buttons that take the user to the next step are usually placed on the bottom left.

The driver envelope in car design has barely changed since the first automobiles were manufactured. Initially vehicles were basic and mechanically focused, but even as they have become more advanced, faster and more technically capable, the sitting position and driving control actions of the driver haven't changed much at all. There may be some minor differences, such as whether the car has an automatic or manual gearbox or whether it is a left-hand or right-hand drive vehicle, but the main human-machine interaction is still the same. A driver can get in any standard car in the world and not have to learn again from scratch how to operate it – a critical factor for road safety.

In the future, we will see driverless cars. This will possibly be the first opportunity to deviate from the conventions of driving design, but conventions hang around a long time, so don't expect them to disappear quickly.

Unfortunately, the manufacturers of showers don't appear to work to an industry convention. Showers typically need only two settings; first, how much water? And second, how hot? So, you would imagine it would be straight forward to create a convention that all showers adhere to. However, manufacturers make them in many different ways, with many different controls.

It's not such a problem for the shower you install in your home - you'll quickly learn how to use it. But when a visitor stays at your home, you've probably heard yourself telling them how to operate the shower. If you travel a lot and stay in different hotels, you'll have undoubtedly experienced the pain of trying to work out how to operate the shower at each new place, and more importantly, how to get it to the setting you want without being covered in cold water.

There's a nice touch by Hotel Brooklyn in Manchester, England, where all guest bathrooms have a hole in the shower enclosure so guests can reach the shower controls from the outside to make sure it's at just the right temperature before they get in.

If you have to create a user manual so customers can use your product, you've already made it too hard for them.

Every single time you fly, you get to experience the safety demonstration. Even if all the passengers have heard it many times before, the flight attendants still go through it, just in case there is a first time flier on board. Every time, with no exceptions.

Everyone knows that!

"Everyone knows you peel a kiwi fruit before you eat it."

"Everyone knows you should press down the clutch pedal before you start the car."

"Everyone knows you need to remove the pedals from a bike before you pack it in a bike case to travel."

"Everyone knows you need to leave the locking wheel nuts available to the mechanic who is servicing your car."

"Everyone knows you shouldn't drink alcohol while taking certain pain killers."

What things in your product or service would you consider to be the obvious - the stuff you assume your customers and your colleagues already know?

What if customers don't already know it?

Chekhov's pistols

You can usually tell in a movie if an object is about to become significant to the storyline. The camera hovers on it just a little too long, or a character interacts with it in a way that draws attention, where previously it wasn't noticed. Similarly, we can sense when the plot is about to take a new twist or turn or change gear. Small clues, like new people or new places, are scattered into the narrative.

Significant objects in a story are known as "Chekhov's pistols". Named after Russian playwright Anton Chekhov, who famously said in a letter, "If you say in the first act that there's a rifle hanging on the wall, in the second act it absolutely must go off. If it's not going to be fired, it shouldn't be hanging there."

It's a beautiful principle of simplicity and keeping things uncomplicated, so that audiences are clear what to expect and don't experience disappointment from not having expectations met. After all, we have all experienced that feeling of closure and resolution when a stage object, or movie prop, identifies its place in the story and its reason for being there. Extra marks if we spotted it early and correctly guessed the plot twist!

Only things relevant to the story should be present, nothing more

"You just need to fill in here... and here... and here... and sign at the bottom."

A slightly embarrassed hotel receptionist apologises for the complexity of the check-in form, and with a quick squiggle of a ball-point pen, they cannibalise the form in front of your eyes, tell you to ignore most of it and highlight the three pieces of information they do actually need you to complete.

(We've all had this experience)

Imagine your product or service is like a stage play. What "props" and "artefacts" do you need to provide to be able to take customers on a journey with you? At what point do you need to introduce each new item or idea to your story, like a Chekhov's pistol? And do you have extra things that aren't relevant just hanging around on set that you can get rid of?

Examples

Asking customers for more information than you need. When Virgin Trains managed the West Coast Mainline Service between Scotland, the North West of England, the West Midlands and London, its online ticket booking system used to ask customers the reason they were buying their train ticket – and it was a compulsory question. The answer never had any impact on the customer's journey.

Giving customers more information than they need. Instruction manuals containing information about all products in a series rather than just the one you bought. Similarly, some manufacturers have one single instruction manual in every possible langauge. Customers get a thick volume in the box, of which they can only read and understand a couple of pages.

Making customers sign in to buy from you. Many ecommerce sites prevent customers from buying products without first creating an account. They also force customers who do have an account but can't remember their password to go through their password reset system rather than let them checkout as a guest.

Making customers work harder than they need to. Budget airlines like Ryanair and Easyjet often make their customers navigate many extra steps online for services they don't want, such as holiday insurance, hire cars and airport extras. Customers can find they unintentionally added something they didn't need to the cost of their trip. They also insist their customers print out their boarding passes at home before they travel, cutting costs on in-person service at the airport and making it a chargable extra. However, customers often end up printing out extra pages of annoying advertising along with their boarding passes.

Making customers look at everything you have for sale! IKEA famously makes its customers walk a one-way path past all of its products in its mega warehouse stores. Unless you are a regular and know the store's shortcuts, you have to walk by everything you don't need to get to the thing you do. (Meaning items you hadn't intended to buy often find themselves in your trolley - we see what you made us do there, IKEA!) Getting round is a Herculean effort, but IKEA knows this and rewards us for succeeding with the offer of super-cheap meatballs and hot dogs at the end.

If you want customers to choose your product or service, you need to put it in the path of least resistance. Have you ever forgotten to complete an important task because you got distracted by other things? Have you intended to call into a shop, but walked right past? Have you received a letter requesting that you phone to book an appointment but you keep forgetting to make that call? Do you have a gym membership or media subscription you no longer use and you intend to cancel it, but never get around to it?

We are not only victims of habit, we are also victims of inertia. We continue to do the default thing. Even the most important tasks can be overlooked because we aren't interrupted and reminded at the right moment. You may think a simple task such as making a phone call is easy, but to complete it, you need to break out of all the other things you are doing.

Changing the default

England and Wales both operate a "deemed consent" system for organ donation. All adults are considered to have opted in to donate their organs in the event of their death, unless they have explicitly opted out.

Before this became law, clinicians, patients and families were left frustrated by the gap between the number of people who said they intended to join the organ donor register and those who were actually on it. An intermediate step of encouraging sign up during an online vehicle duty renewal drew in more donors, but the big win came from changing the system from opt out to opt in. It simply removed the need for people to 'get around' to signing up.

We are victims of inertia...

Posting a letter used to be an everyday thing, but with email, online services, instant messaging and video communication, sending an actual letter in the post now takes a bit more effort. You have to print the letter, find an envelope, pop to the newsagent to buy a packet of stamps and then not only walk by a post box, but remember to take the letter out of your bag and actually put it in the box.

Have you ever carried a letter around with you for several days because you kept forgetting to post it?

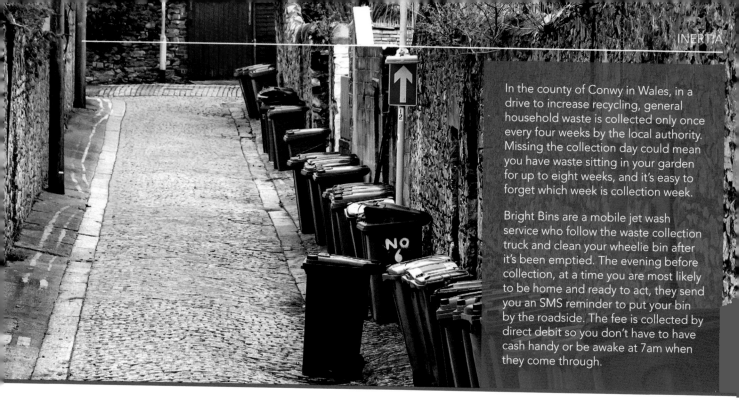

In the county of Conwy in Wales, in a drive to increase recycling, general household waste is collected only once every four weeks by the local authority. Missing the collection day could mean you have waste sitting in your garden for up to eight weeks, and it's easy to forget which week is collection week.

Bright Bins are a mobile jet wash service who follow the waste collection truck and clean your wheelie bin after it's been emptied. The evening before collection, at a time you are most likely to be home and ready to act, they send you an SMS reminder to put your bin by the roadside. The fee is collected by direct debit so you don't have to have cash handy or be awake at 7am when they come through.

Food delivery companies such as Deliveroo and Just Eat make it easier for you to order your favourite restaurant food to eat at home. You don't have to leave the house, you don't even have to leave the sofa, you can just select your meal from an app and wait for it to arrive.

It's no surprise these companies advertise their services throughout the early evening and sponsor primetime evening television programmes. They want to catch you while you are hungry, but also while you are too busy enjoying watching television to want to go out yourself.

Take a look at your customer journey. Can you put the next step in the path of least resistance? For example, enable online transactions and document uploads rather than ask customers to post information to you, and send reminders to them at times they are most likely to take action.

Slow them down

You can lever the power of inertia in the opposite way. If you need customers to pause and carefully consider before they take that next step, then you want to make it less easy.

Every year, UK citizens can take advantage of tax-free savings in an ISA account. There is a limit to how much an individual can save per year and they can only put the money in once. If they draw the money out they can't reuse that allocation so they have to be sure before they draw it.

Similarly, online banking is quick and simple, but it can be costly if we make mistakes. Additional steps in the online journey slow down customers to minimise errors.

Put the next step in the path of least resistance and at a time customers can take action

Bamboozle!

Bamber Boozler poses another 12 questions. Answer using the fastext keys. One wrong and you must try again. Can you answer all 12 in one attempt?

Good day. Let's make it not a blue, but a musical, Monday with a dozen posers covering all styles and tastes. Ready?

Press RED to start

e-mail: bamboozle@teletext.co.uk

GO DIGITAL WITH TELETEXT! p104

P12B   Teletext   12   Jun02 21:08:08

Q1. Composer Marvin Hamlisch is 65 today. He composed the music to which Bond film?

- Diamonds Are Forever
- The Spy Who Loved Me
- Moonraker
- A View to A Kill

As well as cheap holidays (see page 95), news, weather and football scores on Teletext, there was Bamboozle, a quiz programme hosted by a virtual character called "Bamber Boozler". Bamboozle was a series of 12 multiple-choice general knowledge questions, each with four potential answers (selected by the four coloured buttons on the TV remote), and you had to get each one correct to move to the next question. It was a bit like "Who Wants To Be A Millionaire", but a couple of decades earlier. Answering any question wrong bumped players right back right to the start again. There was no way to save your progress or go back one step.

The questions in each game stayed the same, so even if you didn't know the answers, you could guess-and-learn your way through it, but the analogue pages sometimes took a while to load, so getting many of them wrong could lead to a long game.

Getting bumped back to the start again is frustrating. Especially after you've put in time, effort and emotional energy to get to where you are. Have you ever:

- Had to re-sit an exam or resubmit an assignment?

- Had your phone call to a utility company abruptly cut off and you had to go back through the automated answer system again from the beginning?

- Kept your place in a queue with your tip-toes while leaning over to grab an item that is almost out of reach at a supermarket checkout?

- Written a report, but forgot to save it before your computer crashed?

- Completed an online application form, or filled an online shopping basket, only for the internet to 'eat' it and you had to re-do it all again?

- Been passed from department to department and had to explain your issue all over again every time?

No one likes having to go back to the start

REPEAT

In case you don't already know the answer to the question on the previous page is: Green – The Spy Who Loved Me.

No one likes to be kept in suspense either!

"Bamboozle situations"

☐ When patients are readmitted to hospital, they may end up in a different ward or have a different medical team caring for them, and find themselves explaining their recent experience again from the start.

☐ When the same patients face a delay in their medical records being updated and they have to explain it all over again to their G.P. or pharmacist (or paramedic!)

☐ When people face delays awaiting the next steps to resolve a complex problem, and they enquire about the situation, they have to recall everything again from the start.

☐ When departments within an organisation don't talk to each other, leaving the customer frustratingly having to give the back story at each step.

☐ When customers have to start from the beginning yet again when making a formal complaint. (And again when they contact the watchdog or ombudsman.)

☐ When customers hedge their bets by staying on your waiting list, and the waiting lists of your competitors at the same time, so they don't have to start the wait all over again.

Do you have a Bamboozle situation anywhere in your service? How do you help customers track and save their progress? How can you help prevent customers having to go back to the start?

You'd expect that having more choice would be a great thing for consumers. It stands to reason that the more choice we have, the more likely we are to choose something that would be the most perfect for us. We think we want more choice, but in reality, we quickly get overwhelmed when we have too many options to choose between. More options results in suboptimal decision-making, and sometimes no decision at all.

A famous experiment carried out by a team from Columbia and Stanford Universities examined what happened when customers were invited to buy different flavours of jam in a supermarket promotion[28]. When there were just six flavours on offer customers made more purchases than when there were 24 different kinds available.

One of the theories behind why this paradox happens is that of the 'opportunity cost'. The opportunity cost is the price we pay for missing out on the thing we didn't choose. For example, the opportunity cost of a night out having cocktails with friends is all the other things we could have used our time and money for instead, such as time spent at home reading a great novel and money for a new pair of jeans we want to buy. When we are confronted by more possibilities from which to choose, we become more aware of the loss of the options we turned down, and this creates a psychological tension. The easiest way to remove the problem? Don't buy any jam at all.

In practice, it means that having a longer inventory, or menu, of possible products for customers to choose from, the more likely they are to choose none. It's better to keep your products and services focused on a small range of fantastic options. This way, it's more obvious which suits them best. They don't need to feel they are missing out on what they left behind, and they can be happier with their purchase.

Limiting choice may make customers more likely to buy from you...

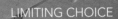

...and feel happier with their purchase

Like many other department stores, Nordstrom stores are typically sprawling shopping spaces covering many thousands of square feet, across many floors.

Having everything you can possibly need all under one roof may make sense on the surface, but few of us want to battle our way through these enormous stores to find the one thing we actually want to buy. Launched in Los Angeles in 2017, Nordstrom tested a new concept store, "Nordstrom Local".

Only 3,000 square feet in size and more like a boutique, the space is much more experiential. Customers pre-select online the products they want to try on, which are brought across town from the regular Nordstrom store in advance. The customer can enjoy a glass of bubbles, maybe get their nails done, and spend time with a personal shopper going through the goods they had pre-selected. The shopping experience becomes less stressful and tiring, and more focused on what the customer actually wants.

Launched in 2010, and now found in locations across the USA, Drybar is a hair salon concept built upon the principle of simplicity. Rather than offer all the different possible combinations of hair cutting, styling and colour, they focus on just one thing, the blow dry, and aim to be the very best at it.

There's an added twist. You can't walk in and describe exactly how you want your hair, you can only choose from a menu of ten styles. They have focused on the best and most popular styles, so even from a menu of ten, you still get to look amazing and on-point at your next career-changing work presentation or big night out.

Keeping the menu to ten styles means they can provide great consistency. The tools and techniques used are the same at each location, meaning you will always get the same quality style, no matter where you book your appointment.

Every time customers have to visit in person, do they have to battle the traffic and find somewhere to park?

P Pay here

What about the cost to customers?

- ☐ Waiting at home for a delivery that should arrive sometime between 7am and 7pm.

- ☐ Taking another day off work because despite waiting in all day, the delivery didn't arrive on the day it should.

- ☐ Having to repeat yourself over and over to different people in different departments.

- ☐ Having to travel through busy traffic and find parking to arrive on time to a scheduled appointment.

- ☐ Waiting on hold for over half an hour to talk to someone in customer support.

- ☐ Having to dispose of pallets and packaging on new appliances.

...being a customer can be exhausting!

When organisations are developing services, they are usually guilty of just seeing the world from their delivery point of view. They write business cases that predict customer need and demand, and calculate the burden to themselves in terms of the delivery cost and effort. For example, the cost of staff, the number of interactions required, the cost of materials and resources, and the cost of product training.

They don't always consider the burden that such a process will put onto customers in terms of how much they will have to reorganise their lives in order to access the products or service in question.

If you are committed to being customer-focused, how can you adjust your experience to minimise the impact and the burden you place on them?

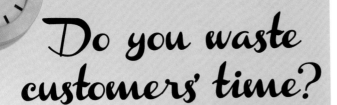

Do you waste customers' time?

Do you leave any 'pause time' in your customer journey? Is there a gap between the time customers commit but haven't actually started yet? Maybe they have signed up to your evening French classes but your next course only starts in five weeks time.

Can you somehow keep customers engaged while they wait to get started? Is there a way for them to use this time to get a head start instead?

Do you waste people's time? On hold on the telephone, in queues, sitting in waiting rooms? Can you make the experience of waiting better? More entertaining? More interesting? Educational maybe? Less awful at least. (And magazines from last year don't count!)

Do you make people waste time reading your FAQs before you'll help them?

Looks like you're going to be waiting a while!

long wait ahead...

Do customers have to wait for you to get your act together and organise something before they can move forward? For example, do you need to organise a meeting, or get a team together before the next step can happen?

A common example of this kind of delay is experienced by older people who are medically ready to leave hospital but who end up staying many days longer while a range of professionals carry out assessments on their homes.

"Who writes like this?"

Have you ever enjoyed a work of fiction so much that you went back to the book store to get another volume written by the same author? Let's imagine you enjoyed that book just as much. Soon, you may find you have worked your way through the author's whole catalogue, and then what can you do?

Assuming you want more of the same, you may want to know who writes like them. Before book ownership was so popular, most people borrowed books from the lending library. "Who writes like…" was a common question asked to librarians from people finding a genre they enjoyed, and looking for inspiration for their next good read. Initiatives to connect readers to authors started in the public library system decades ago. Then, over time, as more of us have become book owners, and the book selling industry has seen such huge growth, these systems have developed and matured and are now the mega-data-driven algorithms you can expect to find powering recommendations to customers on platforms such as Amazon and Audible.

Netflix builds a profile of all its customers, based on the simple assumption that if they continue to watch a series or movie beyond its beginning then they must be enjoying it. Collecting viewing data from millions of customers across many countries has enabled it to make data-led decisions on the kind of series and content it should commission, because it can predict whether it will be a raging success or not. If you preview a movie, Netflix will give you a "% match" score of how much it believes the movie in question fits with your previous viewing activity.

Most large online retailers give you recommendations on items to buy based on your browsing and purchasing behaviour and the behaviour of others who have bought similar products to you. Need to buy new specialist light bulbs for your new ceiling lamp? Or need to know which bracket is the right one for your new radiator? No problem. They will also tell you at point of purchase which compatible extras you need and make it easy for you to add them to your basket.

When we try to persuade people to buy from us or to take a course of action, we can fall into the trap of telling them how easy it is, even when it's not. People are motivated to act when the expected benefits they will get outweigh the cost and effort of their actions. As we instinctively know this, we can be guilty of trying to diminish the cost and effort, to nudge them over that threshold so they will make that purchase, take action, or at least take the first few steps.

You will have heard yourself and others say things like "but it's so easy, anyone can do it", "it only takes a few minutes a day", "you'll love it, and it's so easy to do", "it's easy to get signed up, all you have to do is…", "it's never been easier to…"

However, there is a pitfall to this approach. Often, the thing isn't easy. Any kind of lifestyle change is hard because it requires the breaking of habits and the forming of new ones, which takes time and repetition. Many processes that on the outside seem simple enough can still be stressful.

If you talk about how accessing your products and services is so easy, and your customers actually find it difficult, they will become frustrated and disengaged when the reality doesn't meet their expectations.

Remember, it's a balance. It doesn't have to be easy. Your customer just has to believe it is worth the cost and effort. If you know it won't be straight forward for them, can you instead focus on the expected benefits and how good they are?

Talking about the amazing benefits is better than saying it's easy. (Though better to make it as easy as possible for them anyway!)

It's easy

Tell us how worthwhile it is

We're talking about this quadrant here

Desirable

Frustration   Engagement

Disinterest   Apathy

Easy

> 66 This won't be the easiest thing you've ever done, but the benefits are so amazing, you'll be so happy you did it. 99

It's so good it's worth the effort

Sometimes, a product is undesirable, or we want it to be undesirable, but it's just too easy.

Globally, Uber has faced continuing storms about the terms and conditions under which its drivers work and the amount of corporate tax it pays. We say, "I don't want to use Uber anymore." But... the ride experience is still great, the app is easy and convenient and there's a car in our neighbourhood when we need to go somewhere.

Small, local, independent retailers desperately need our custom to survive. They don't have the might and the power and the resilience of the big firms. We say, "I'm going to support local." But then we want an item they can't get in stock for another two days, and Amazon will deliver it to our door before 10pm tonight.

Ryanair rattles us with outlandish announcements about changes to the passenger experience. It says it'll reduce the size of carry-on bags, if it could it'd charge us to use the onboard toilet and it'd like to introduce "standing-only seats", if only the Civil Aviation Authority would allow it. (All true!) We say, "I won't fly Ryanair again." But then our friend is getting married in a beautiful Spanish castle and it's the only way we can get there.

What happens if your brand is undesirable, but your products are needed and you have made your processes so efficient and easy for customers...?

The fact we continue to buy from brands we don't necessarily like shows the power of offering an easy and efficient service.

It may, therefore, seem a good strategy to plough all of your resources and effort into making your service easy for customers, even if they don't really like you. That is, until an equally easy rival brand shows up that they like more...

We continue to buy from brands we don't really like, because it's too convenient

Facebook started in 2004 and Twitter in 2006. That makes them teenagers now. Despite earlier attempts at touchscreen devices, the one that changed everything was the first Apple iPhone, back in 2007. To put this another way, we now have a generation of young adults who have never experienced anything other than having this technology and these platforms as part of their everyday lives. They cannot remember a time in the past before these products existed.

Digital technology is changing everything fast. Can you remember a time when in order to access the internet, you had to go to the room in your house where the desktop computer was connected to the router? And you had to listen to the high-pitched, crackly dial-up sound as it connected. Can you remember when mobile phones only had enough capacity to store ten SMS messages?

Websites used to be like magazines, containing information only. Then they became transactional, enabling customers to make bookings and purchases, and to connect with each other. Now, they are transformational - you can manage almost your whole life through digital products. You can order your groceries for delivery, stream movies and music, take part in online yoga, and collaborate with colleagues from all over the world on work projects. All before lunch.

Digital technology has been a game changer for industries and their customers alike. Customers have been allowed to engage at a time and in a way that is most convenient to them. They have benefitted from the redistribution of power and information into their hands. As previously covered in this book, no longer do we have to go to a travel agent to get the best flight deals. We can find an apartment to rent for a week in a city thousands of miles away. We can book an Uber and watch on our screens as it travels across town to collect us. We can find a parked Evo Car and drive it away for the day. We can instantly download millions of books to read or listen to. We can put a GPS tag on our dog's collar and never again have to worry we won't find them if they escape the back yard or run off during exercise. Notifications of important breaking news shows up on our phone screens.

As citizens around the world were ordered to stay at home during the Covid-19 pandemic, we quickly learned how to successfully work remotely and connect with each other using video call technology and online collaboration tools. At scale! Clinicians moved to online patient consultations. Courts services started offering online hearings in legal cases.

With global travel all but halted in 2020 and tourism industries everywhere suffering, a number of Caribbean islands offered special extended visas for visitors who wished to relocate and work remotely from their island for the year. Packages included special long-stay rates, free wifi, and cheap sim cards, so that visitors could work comfortably.

The world is constantly changing, and it will continue to do so. Digital technology will continue to transform our lives.

Almost no services will remain 100% analogue in future

Consider how the use of digital technology can improve your product or service, make it more efficient, make it easier or make it more accessible for customers. And then do it again. By the time you have implemented your initial ideas, the world will have moved on and there will be a new edge…

Fancy conducting your remote working life for the next year from the Bahamas?

Online, in person, by telephone, on Twitter, via Skype, by post, online chat, email, text message... we all have our preferred method of communicating with others. And those preferences change too, based on the circumstance, time of day, urgency, or even just our mood.

If you're idly looking for inspiration for a new outfit, you may start online rather than take a walk down the high street, but then you may prefer to try and buy in a store. If you're making an enquiry about car insurance, you'll probably also start online, but quickly move to telephone if you find that what you need is too complex for the online system. Many people don't like making phone calls in the evening, or indeed any time of day.

Do you do your banking face to face, or do you prefer to use an app for that? Do you like to pour over paper brochures received by post for things like holidays and electronic equipment, or do you keep a tab open on your browser so you can have a look whenever you get a spare few minutes?

What are your own preferred channels of communication?

The more channels you have available for people to be able to reach you, the more comfortable you make it for them to engage with you. How many channels do you make available for your customers, and are there any you don't have that you should be considering?

in person

by post

by phone   online

Many organisations play with the channels they offer for their own convenience, rather than the convenience of their customers. For example, they may shut down web chat if it's getting busy, tell customers already on the phone they have to go online, or hide their phone number and send customers to the FAQ knowledge bank instead.

Stop sending customers to your FAQs!

It may be efficient for you, maybe even for them, but it leaves a lasting impression that you don't care, and you are happy for them to do the hard work to answer their own questions, so you don't have to.

It's about their convenience, not your convenience!

Every New Year, moments of intense celebration roll in around the globe, starting in New Zealand and Australia, and then time zone by time zone, as all the nations of the world spin across the moment of midnight. Scenes of celebrations are broadcast from major cities like Tokyo, Dubai, Paris, London, New York and San Francisco.

Have you ever stopped to wonder why all the time zones in the world are compared to GMT, Greenwich Mean Time? GMT (also known as Coordinated Universal Time, or UTC) is the zero point for standard time. All other time zones are described based on their geographical distance from Greenwich, London. For example, Pacific Coast Time is GMT-8 hours.

But why is Greenwich the home of standard time? Why the United Kingdom? Why not anywhere else in the world?

It turns out that the United Kingdom was the first place to have a universal time system, with all towns and villages across the length and breadth of the country operating the exact same time.

Originally, the time of day was measured by the sundial, which traced the sun across the daytime sky, rising in the east, setting in the west. The time of day, therefore, varied ever so slightly from town to city to village across the country, based on how far east-west (and north-south) they were. Towns west of London lagged slightly behind, those east of London were slightly ahead. Towns and cities proudly shared their local time with their communities through large clocks mounted in church steeples and town halls.

But this was all set to change in 1840, and it was all because of the railways.

The UK became the first nation to have a national railway system connecting its towns and cities. A universal time system became a necessity for two reasons. Firstly, to keep trains running safely and separated from each other, and secondly, to ensure passengers, railway staff and signalmen accurately knew the time of train arrivals and departures. It was known as "Railway Time" and it began in 1840, but for the first few years it was confined just to the railway. Railway staff carried small books of tables that translated the time between their local time and railway time. However, despite huge resistance, Railway Time slowly became the adopted time nationwide. (Special mention goes to Liverpool, for leading the way.) Greenwich, which already had a global presence monitoring maritime activity, became the new zero location of time.

a whole nation literally changed time

Many of our modern services and processes require high levels of partnership working, and adherence to design standards and conventions for interoperability and consistency. Adopting these systems may be painful, and require a lot of compromise. But, next time you find yourself thinking that it's too hard to do, just remember that there was a time when, in the spirit of progress, a whole nation literally changed time.

☐ Map out your customer journey. Plot all the times that a customer comes into contact with your service. Include all real-world and online interactions and transactions, every form that needs to be completed and all follow up support. Do you think there are too many steps? Can you reduce the number of steps the customer has to take?

☐ Can you join together or eliminate any of the stages of the customer journey to make it easier? (Easier for the customer – not for you!)

☐ At every stage in the customer journey, do you tell them what happens next and what to expect? Can you provide a better experience by telling them what they should bring with them at each stage?

☐ Are there any aspects of your product or service that customers find confusing or intimidating? If so, do one of four things... 1. Simplify, 2. Provide more support, 3. Do it for them, or 4. Eliminate it.

☐ If you want to encourage people to choose your product or service over another, you need to put it in the path of least resistance. Can you take the service nearer to your customers or embed the journey into other areas of their lives to help them overcome inertia?

☐ Do you make it difficult for people to understand what your product or service is? Would it pass the four tests? (Explain what you do to a small child, to an elderly relative, without talking, or to a Martian!)

☐ Can you use the laws of affordance to design products and services that customers intuitively know how to use and navigate?

☐ Does your sector operate with conventions you need to use? Conventions are designed systems, like keyboards, handheld devices and highway signage, that are so widely used they become the 'industry standard'. Going against a convention makes it harder for a customer to use your product.

- If you say it's easy when it isn't, people will become frustrated and disengaged because reality didn't meet their expectations. If your service is hard to access, are you telling your customers how worthwhile it is instead?

- Using the "Chekhov's Pistol" principle, do you only include steps in your journey, or ask for customer information, that is absolutely essential?

- How many channels do you use to allow people to communicate with you? Online, Twitter, Facebook, SMS, email, telephone, in-person. Do you actively close off channels to customers, for example by making it hard for them to call you on the phone? Are you making it easy for people to reach you using their chosen method? Do not send customers to your online FAQ!

- Don't expect customers to hunt around to find what they are looking for. Are you making it easy for them to get straight to the information they want?

- If customers visit you in real life how can you make it easier for them to find you? For example, give details of where they can park, and the location of the nearest bus stop.

- Can you make decisions easier for customers by limiting choice? It may sound counterintuitive, but too many options to choose from can be debilitating and require a lot of cognitive effort. As long as the options are good ones, customers will be happy to have the decision they make made simpler.

- Do you want people to keep hold of information you give them? Can you make it "sticky" by connecting it with something useful?

- Do you bump customers back to the start again? Do you operate an online service that has a time out after which they go back to the start? Do you send customers from department to department and they have to wait in line each time and explain themselves all over again?

- Do you make customers wait? Waiting on the day, in a queue, in a waiting room, on hold on the phone. Do you make them wait in the overall customer journey, waiting for an engineer, or a letter, or a delivery? How can you minimise the amount of time they spend waiting?

- Is there anything you believe is common knowledge, which you assume your customers know already, but they don't? Make sure you are not making their lives difficult by excluding important information you think they already have.

- Can you help customers find products they are looking for by making recommendations based on their preferences and history?

- Consider the rise of digital over the last couple of decades. It now touches on almost every aspect of life. Customers expect to be able to engage with products and services digitally and find it frustrating if they can't. In what way do you need to evolve your digital presence to continue to meet the needs and wants of your customers?

Index

Images

All photographs Getty Images unless credited below:

Phillip Hampson   Blackpool Tower Ballroom (page 18)
Kris Williams   Glyder Fach, Snowdonia (pages 66 & 67)
Teletext   Holidays and Bamboozle (pages 95 & 184)
Google Maps   screen image (page 97)
Katherine Benjamin   Ski Racer (page 111)
James Jones   New York City (page 148)
Denise Hampson   Love, Love, Love (page 25)
      The Heineken Experience, Amsterdam (page 73)
      Emirates Aviation Experience, London (page 73)
      SONOS, New York City (page 73)
      Stamps Landing, Vancouver (page 79)
      Bakerloo Line, London Underground (page 97)
      Dyson Store, London (page 116)
      New York City (pages 148 & 149)
      lululemon, 5th Avenue, New York City (page 150)
      All images page 151
      John Fleuvog Shoes, Vancouver (page 160)
      Hyde Park Corner, London (pages 172 & 173)

All illustrations by Denise Hampson unless credited below:

Getty Images -   Roulette wheel (page 104)
      Playing cards (page 104)
      Seagull (page 106)

Book written and designed by Denise Hampson

References

1   Department of Health, 2011. *Healthy Lives, Healthy People: A call to action on obesity in England.*

2   National Survey for Wales 2019-20: Adult Lifestyle. (2020). [online] Gov Wales. Available at: https://gov.wales/sites/default/files/statistics-and-research/2020-07/adult-lifestyle-national-survey-wales-april-2019-march-2020-390.pdf

3   Kahneman, D., 2012. *Thinking, Fast and Slow.* London: Penguin. pp.19-30.

4, 5   Social Bakers. Twitter statistics - Brands. [online] Available at: https://www.socialbakers.com/statistics/twitter/profiles/brands

6   Kilner, J. and Lemon, R., 2013. What We Know Currently about Mirror Neurons. *Current Biology,* 23(23), pp.R1057-R1062.

7   Cherry, E., 1953. Some Experiments on the Recognition of Speech, with One and with Two Ears. *The Journal of the Acoustical Society of America,* 25(5), pp.975-979.

8   Sedikides, C., Wildschut, T., Arndt, J. and Routledge, C., 2008. Nostalgia. *Current Directions in Psychological Science,* 17(5), pp.304-307.

9   Thaler, R. H., 1981. Some Empirical Evidence on Dynamic Inconsistency. *Economics Letters.* 8(3), pp.201–207

10   Macrotrends. U.K. Life Expectancy 1950-2021. [online] Available at: https://www.macrotrends.net/countries/GBR/united-kingdom/life-expectancy

11   Hershfield, H., 2011. Future self-continuity: how conceptions of the future self transform intertemporal choice. *Annals of the New York Academy of Sciences,* 1235(1), pp.30-43.

12   Tversky, A. and Kahneman, D., 1973. Availability: A heuristic for judging frequency and probability. *Cognitive Psychology,* 5(2), pp.207-232.

13   Tversky, A. and Kahneman, D., 1971. Belief in the law of small numbers. *Psychological Bulletin,* 76(2), pp.105-110.

14   Kahneman, D., 2012. *Thinking, Fast and Slow.* London: Penguin. pp.277-288.

15   Darwin, C., 1871. Courtship, Intersexual Selection, and Intrasexual Competition: The Hot Ape. Geher, G., 2013. *Evolutionary Psychology 101,* pp.56-57.

16   Zajonc, R., 1968. Attitudinal effects of mere exposure. *Journal of Personality and Social Psychology,* 9(2, Pt.2), pp.1-27.

17   Helix Sleep. Sleep Quiz. [online] Available at: https://helixsleep.com/pages/get-personalized

18   Buell, W. R., 2018. Last Place Aversion in Queues. *Harvard Business Review,* pp.9-11.

19   Taylor, D. M. and Doria, J. R., 1981. Self-serving and group-serving bias in attribution. *Journal of Social Psychology,* 113(2), pp.201-211.

20   Kahneman, D., 2012. *Thinking, Fast and Slow.* London: Penguin. pp.377-385.

21   Kahneman, D., Fredrickson, B., Schreiber, C. and Redelmeier, D., 1993. When More Pain Is Preferred to Less: Adding a Better End. *Psychological Science,* 4(6), pp.401-405.

22   Shapiro, B. and Wax, N., 2018. *What We Keep.* 1st ed. New York: Running Press Book Publishers.

23   Net Promoter Network. [online] Available at: https://www.netpromoter.com/

24   Miller, D. and Ross, M., 1975. Self-serving biases in the attribution of causality: Fact or fiction? *Psychological Bulletin,* 82(2), pp.213-225.

25   Isen, A., Rosenzweig, A. and Young, M., 1991. The Influence of Positive Affect on Clinical Problem solving. *Medical Decision Making,* 11(3), pp.221-227.

26   Ministry of Justice, 2012. Public sector equality duty. [online] Available at: https://www.gov.uk/government/publications/public-sector-equality-duty

27   UK Government. Design System. [online] Available at: https://design-system.service.gov.uk/

28   Iyengar, S. and Lepper, M., 2000. When choice is demotivating: Can one desire too much of a good thing? *Journal of Personality and Social Psychology,* 79(6), pp.995-1006.

DENISE HAMPSON

Denise is a Behavioural Economics and Experience Design Consultant. She has worked with hundreds of organisations in the UK and North America, in a career shaped by curiosity (and coffee) and her unique view of the world.

She has spoken at many high-profile events and conferences, including TEDx, SXSW, Interface Health and Technology Summit and the UK House of Lords.

Between 1999 and 2004, Denise was a member of the highly successful Great Britain Track Cycling Team, and she is a past British Women's Sprint Champion and British 200m record holder.

Prior to her athletic career, Denise was a Systems Engineer at BAE Systems, specialising in human-system interaction and cockpit design on the Eurofighter Typhoon. This is what started her career-long obsession with human-centred design and creating systems and services that are best matched to real human behaviour.

Denise enjoys cycling in good weather, running in bad weather, and drinking coffee with interesting people (regardless of the weather).

@DeniseHampson

create
amazing
experiences